What Connected Educators Do Differently

What Connected Educators Do Differently

Todd Whitaker
Jeffrey Zoul
Jimmy Casas

First published 2015
by Routledge
711 Third Avenue, New York, NY 10017

and by Routledge
2 Park Square, Milton Park, Abingdon, Oxon OX14 4RN

Routledge is an imprint of the Taylor & Francis Group, an
informa business

Library of Congress Cataloging-in-Publication Data

Whitaker, Todd, 1959–
    What connected educators do differently / Todd Whitaker, Jeff
Zoul, Jimmy Casas.
        pages cm
    Includes bibliographical references.
    1. Teachers—Professional relationships.   2. Teaching.   I. Zoul, Jeffrey.
II. Title.
    LB1775.W437 2015
    371.102—dc23
    2014036367

ISBN: 978-1-138-83200-8 (pbk)
ISBN: 978-1-315-73625-9 (ebk)

Typeset in WarnockPro
by Apex CoVantage, LLC

The authors would like to dedicate this book to
the following people . . .

*To my mother, Avis Whitaker, who is one of the most
connected people I know.*

Todd

*To my daughter, Lina Alvarez, who serves as a model
of connected learning and living.*

Jeff

*To my three children, Alexio (AJ), Miraya, and Marisa,
who motivate me and inspire me to give my best
to others every day.*

Jimmy

Contents

▶ **Key Connector 7**

▶ **Key Connector 8**

eResources

On our website, you'll find two eResources that accompany the book—a hyperlinked list of the urls mentioned in this book, and a bonus list of Edchats available by state. These eResources are available for free download.

You can access these downloads by visiting the book product page on our website http://www.routledge.com/books/details/9781138832008. Then click on the tab that says "eResources," and select the files. They will begin downloading to your computer.

Meet the Authors

▶ **Dr. Todd Whitaker** has been fortunate to blend his passion with his career. Recognized as a leading presenter in the field of education, his message about the importance of teaching has resonated with hundreds of thousands of educators around the world. Todd is a professor of educational leadership at Indiana State University in Terre Haute, Indiana, and he has spent his life pursuing his love of education by researching and studying effective teachers and principals.

Prior to moving into higher education, he was a math teacher and basketball coach in Missouri. Todd then served as a principal at the middle school, junior high, and high school levels. He was also a middle school coordinator in charge of staffing, curriculum, and technology for the opening of new middle schools.

One of the nation's leading authorities on staff motivation, teacher leadership, and principal effectiveness, Todd has written over 30 books including the national bestseller, *What Great Teachers Do Differently*. Other titles include: *Shifting the Monkey, Dealing With Difficult Teachers, The Ten-Minute Inservice, The Ball, What Great Principals Do Differently, Motivating and Inspiring Teachers*, and *Dealing With Difficult Parents*. Please follow and contact Todd via Twitter: @ToddWhitaker.

▶ **Dr. Jeffrey Zoul** is a lifelong teacher, learner, and leader, currently serving as Assistant Superintendent for Teaching and Learning with Deerfield

Public Schools District 109 in Deerfield, Illinois. Prior to working in this capacity, Jeff served as a district administrator in Rock Island, Illinois, and a school improvement specialist with the Southern Regional Education Board (SREB), the nation's largest and oldest non-profit school improvement network. Jeff also served as a principal with Forsyth County Schools in Cumming, Georgia, and with North Shore School District 112 in Highland Park, Illinois. Before serving as an administrator, Dr. Zoul was a classroom teacher for 18 years in the state of Georgia, teaching elementary school, middle school, and high school English.

Dr. Zoul is also the author of several books, including *Improving Your School One Week at a Time: Building the Foundation for Professional Teaching and Learning* and *4 CORE Factors for School Success*, co-authored with Dr. Todd Whitaker. Jeff has also served as an adjunct professor at North Georgia College and State University, teaching graduate level courses in Research and Assessment. In 2014, he was awarded the Bammy Educators' Voice Award as the School Business Official of the Year.

Dr. Zoul earned a BA degree in Education from the University of Massachusetts at Amherst and a Master of Science degree in Education from Troy University, Alabama. In addition, he earned an Education Specialist's degree from the University of Southern Mississippi and a doctoral degree from the University of Alabama in Tuscaloosa, Alabama. Please follow and contact Jeff via Twitter: @Jeff_Zoul.

▶   **Jimmy Casas** is in his 21st year of administrative leadership. He received his BA in Spanish and Master's in Teaching from the University of Iowa and his Master's in Administrative Leadership from Cardinal Stritch University in Milwaukee. He is currently pursuing his EdS at the University of Iowa.

Jimmy has served as principal at Bettendorf High School in Bettendorf, Iowa, for the last 13 years. Prior to moving into administration, he served as a Spanish teacher in Milwaukee public schools. An experienced administrator at both the middle and high school levels, Jimmy brings a vast knowledge and understanding of school improvement reform initiatives, critical changes required to improve academic performance for all students, and the positive impact shared leadership has on school climate and the educational process. His passion for teaching and learning, coupled with a vision for developing a community of leaders, have helped to produce a culture of excellence and high standards for both students and staff. Mr. Casas is a sought-after speaker and trainer at local, state, and national levels.

Jimmy was named the 2012 Iowa Secondary Principal of the Year and was selected as one of three finalists for NASSP 2013 National Secondary Principal of the Year. In 2013, he was awarded the Bammy Educators' Voice Award as the Secondary School Principal of the Year in 2012. He co-founded EdCampIowa in 2012, providing a self-led professional development format for all educators and community members. Mr. Casas is the co-founder and co-oderator of #IAedchat, on Twitter, moderating the online discussion chat every Sunday at 8:00 a.m. and p.m. CST. Please follow and contact Jimmy via Twitter: @casas_jimmy.

Acknowledgments

Our interest in writing this book is the direct result of having been profoundly and positively impacted by the members of our personal and professional learning networks. It could not have been written without their support, wisdom, insights, and modeling. We consider ourselves fortunate indeed to be connected to thousands of educators around the world who are giants in our profession and we wish to acknowledge their contributions in making this book a reality. Many of these educators are referenced by name within the pages of this book; to those educators, we are grateful for your inspiration. To the thousands of others whose contributions were equally impactful, but whose names are missing herein, we salute you as well.

In addition to acknowledging the important contributions of our extended learning networks, we also wish to acknowledge the following people for ongoing support above and beyond what one should reasonably expect: Jimmy wants to express his deepest appreciation to the administrative and secretarial team at Bettendorf High School for their support, including Joy Kelly, Kevin Skillett, Kristy Cleppe, Colin Wikan, Sarah Peakin, and Kathy Ouellette as well as the entire faculty and staff for their commitment to excellence. Their passion, pride, and support for all students are both admired and appreciated. Jeff wishes to acknowledge the amazing educators serving in Deerfield (IL) Public Schools District 109 who work tirelessly on a daily basis to connect the most important people of all—our students—to the world of learning that surrounds them.

Finally, the authors wish to acknowledge the contributions and support of the team at Routledge Press, including Lauren Davis, whose close reading and editing of the manuscript and insightful suggestions improved it immensely.

Getting Connected: What it Means and Why it Matters

The best time to plant a tree is twenty years ago. The second best time is now.

Ancient proverb

The fact that you are reading a book about connected educators written by these three authors is, in itself, a testament to the power of becoming a *connected* educator in the 21st century. None of us is a "digital native" and, in fact, each of us is at a chronological age somewhat north of the typical connected educator we meet around the world, both in person and via online formats. Collectively, we have served the education profession for nearly 90 years; yet, instead of slowing down, we find ourselves more energized than ever before about our noble profession of teaching, learning, and leadership. Much of this energy comes from the intentional decision we each made separately—but nearly simultaneously—to reach beyond the scope of the traditional connections we had made over the course of our careers in education to a broader network around the world. The platform that started each of us moving in this direction was Twitter—something we discuss in some detail in several chapters of this book—but what we started to learn as we began our individual journeys, connecting with educators in new ways in locations both near and far, is something that Todd wrote about in his previous bestselling books, *What Great Principals Do Differently* (2002) and *What Great Teachers Do Differently* (2004). There are specific things that great principals and great teachers do that set them apart from others. Likewise, differences exist between connected educators in the 21st century and those less connected. Whether looking at principals, teachers, or connected educators, these differences lie not in what they *know*, but in what they *do*.

This book is about what connected educators do that sets them apart from their less-connected colleagues, helping them to perform more effectively and efficiently as a result. As these variables were explored, we leaned not so much on scholarly research, but, instead, on what we ourselves were learning about and from other connected teachers, administrators, professors, and educational leaders we met in our daily efforts and about how to connect with them. One key learning we took away applies to the quotation that introduces this chapter: the time for educators to start connecting to a larger personal learning network—if you did not already embark upon this 20 years ago—is now. There is simply too much to be gained—and nothing to lose—to not begin connecting with educators around the world who share your passion about this noble profession that is education.

We have met many educators in many roles around the world who have expressed an interest in getting connected beyond their local network of colleagues, but who have also lamented that it was too late in their career to get started or had some other hesitation about getting started. To anyone who may feel this way, please know that each of us also felt this way before we eventually reached out in new ways to establish a new and improved personal learning network of professional colleagues. In fact, each of us initially resisted the idea of reaching out at all, beyond what was our comfort zone. Each of us was very successful in our more traditional way of thinking, working, and communicating. We worked hard at our day jobs, attended conferences regularly, presented to audiences whenever possible, published books and articles, sent emails to educators around the world whom we had met in person, and talked to fellow educators on the phone whenever possible. Truthfully, we still do all these things as a way to connect and learn with people we respect. That is one of the key tenets of this book: being a connected educator does not mean we no longer connect in traditional ways such as those described above. We take the view that truly connected educators connect in a wide variety of ways, never losing sight of the fact that no amount of online connectivity can replace connecting face to face. Having said that, we have found that connecting in new ways—many of which we will share throughout this book—has made us more

effective, more knowledgeable, more energized, and more efficient as professional educators.

▶ CONNECTED EDUCATORS DEFINED

Our primary purpose in writing this book was to identify what
it is, precisely, that connected educators do differently from
those who are not and how we can share these practices with
other educators wishing to connect. We aim to align these practices with specific strategies for fulfilling each. We have had
numerous conversations, both in face-to-face settings and in a
multitude of online settings, to discuss and even debate what it
means to be a connected educator.

Jimmy is the founder and co-moderator of Iowa Edchat, an
hour-long weekly discussion among educators that convenes
every Sunday morning and evening throughout the year. In a
June 2014 Sunday morning edition of Iowa Edchat (known as
#IAedchat on Twitter (we write in detail about educational
"chats" on Twitter and how they can serve as a tremendous
resource and support for all educators in a subsequent chapter), participants were asked to explain their views on what
it means to be a connected educator. The responses stand as
an interesting way to kick off the conversation in this book.
A few of the insightful and helpful responses included the
following (we have included both the name of the responder
as well as their Twitter "handle"—again, this is something
we discuss at length in subsequent chapters of this book, but
for now, please note that due to character limits, educators
on Twitter use many abbreviations, including some you see
below):

- Dan Butler @danpbutler: Being connected means developing relationships with many through the use of tech
  tools to enhance our work.
- John Fritzky @JohnFritzy: Being connected means developing relationships with experts in many different fields
  of education.
- Devin Schoening @dschoening: Being connected means
  having access to real people anywhere in the world. Also
  means there is a give and take. Not just take.

- Nathan Lang, EdD @nalang1: A dynamic view of education. Doesn't view our work as procedural, but as work that requires continual revision & reflection.
- Jon Harper @Jonharper70bd: It means opening ourselves up to voices other than the ones inside our heads. I don't get any smarter listening to myself think.
- Jennifer Brittin @jenbrittin: Learning happens beyond the four walls of the classroom for Ts and Ss ("Ts" and "Ss" refers to "Teachers" and "Students").
- Ryan Huels @huels_ryan: One who is committed to improving their craft by reaching out to S, P, and educators by whatever means possible ("S" and "P" refer to "Students" and "Parents").
- Kyle Engdahl @engdkyl: To be connected is to seek answers to questions, find support from others, & build a community to help and challenge yourself.
- Shaelynn Farnsworth @shfarnsworth: Connected Educator—Utilizing various modes to learn and share. Broadening knowledge and reach to best serve students.
- Aaron Becker @Aaron_Becker32: Prioritizing time to reach out to educators around the world to continually make you better at what you do for kids.

The above comments were taken directly from the participants' "tweets" as they responded to questions posed to them by the chat's moderators (you can find an archive of the entire hour-long chat at https://storify.com/danpbutler/iaedchat-am-edition-the-connected-educator).

Based on our experiences talking with educators around the world like the ones we highlighted from this recent chat, we have identified eight key things that educators do that make the case for them being connected. These "key connectors" are, of course, what form the bulk of this book and which, we hope, will help anyone reading this book maximize their professional and personal lives as educators by becoming more connected. Although we go into great detail about each of these eight keys in remaining chapters, for now, it may help to present our own definition of what it means to be a connected educator.

Being a connected educator is not a formal title, of course; there is no degree program or certification process one goes through to be deemed a connected educator. Our view is that serving as a connected educator is a mindset more than anything else; a connected educator tends to adopt and live out a mindset that believes:

- Educators can leverage online communities of practice to improve their effectiveness and enhance student learning.
- Educators can and should establish networks to share practices, access experts, and solve problems.
- Educators become connected "educators" by first becoming connected and constant "learners," ones who reach out to learn, share, and collaborate with a network of fellow learners interested in education.
- Educators must collaborate in a variety of ways, including online, using social media to interact with colleagues from around the globe, engaging in conversations in safe online places, and bringing what they learn back to their classrooms, schools, districts, universities, and organizations.
- Educators must not look down on their colleagues, nor suggest that the "average" classroom is somehow broken. They seek only to grow professionally through continuous improvement.
- Educators must live not just as readers or viewers, but as active participants in ongoing discussions, planning, and problem solving.
- Educators can have access to a large collective brain trust consisting of diverse ideas and perspectives.
- Educators must use technology and social media to individualize their learning for both personal and professional growth.

In short, we define connected educators simply as ones who are actively and constantly seeking new opportunities and resources to grow as professionals. In the subsequent pages of this book we hope to share practical, commonsense ways to learn and grow by taking specific actions to maximize such opportunities and resources.

▶ SHARING OUR OWN STORY

We think it important to share our own story of how we became more connected as educators. Throughout this book, we provide examples of how we connect with other educators around the world to learn from each other. We also think it is important to share how the three of us became connected and how over time our professional connection grew into a personal connection as well. We think it typifies the stories of many other educators we have encountered who initially "meet" via Twitter or some other social media network when discussing some aspect of our profession. Often, this initial meeting leads to many other exchanges; over time, such educators often meet face to face eventually and find that they have much in common as educators—and as human beings—and wind up becoming "networked" both professionally and personally. In Chapter 1, we focus on the foundation of becoming a connected educator, which is simply to grow what is known as a "Personal Learning Network" (PLN). We have also seen this referred to as a "Professional Learning Network." We maintain that connected educators focus on creating and maintaining both personal *and* professional networks, resulting in even more powerful relationships, to create what we like to call P^{2}LNs, with "P to the power of 2" representing personal and professional (we refer to these learning networks as "PLNs" and "P^{2}LNs" interchangeably throughout this book).

So how did the three of us become connected personally and professionally? Jeff and Todd have known each other for over a decade and worked on many projects together in that time. However, our relationship with Jimmy is more recent and began in a way that, again, we think is both powerful and revealing about how educators are beginning to connect and collaborate in new ways in the 21st century. When Jeff was serving as an assistant superintendent in Rock Island, Illinois, he organized an inaugural "Teaching and Learning Conference" in his district. This was a full-day offering of professional learning sessions from which educators in his district could choose several to attend. Although the bulk of the session presenters were teachers and administrators serving in the district, Jeff did invite a few colleagues he had come to know and respect via

Twitter to present as well. One such outside presenter, Nancy Blair (@blairteach), arrived a day early for the conference simply so she could meet Jimmy Casas—someone she had never before met or spoken to, yet someone she had grown to know and respect greatly, also through Twitter exchanges. Jimmy lives and works across the Mississippi from Rock Island, in Bettendorf, Iowa. When Nancy contacted Jimmy via Twitter, asking if she could meet him and see his school when she was in the area, Jimmy was mildly surprised because, again, he and Nancy had never met in person or spoken on the phone. At this time, Jimmy was just beginning to actively connect as an educator through Twitter and other avenues. Still, he immediately invited Nancy to stop by his school that Sunday morning for a tour of the campus, followed by breakfast. Nancy called Jeff to invite him along. When Jeff learned from Nancy that plans were made for the three of them to visit Bettendorf High School, he was not exactly thrilled. Meeting a person he had never before met, and assumed he would never meet again, for a tour of the school and breakfast, was not something high on his priority list, and he even asked Nancy to go alone so he could spend the entire day preparing for the conference taking place on Monday. Thankfully for Jeff, Nancy insisted he go along. The morning proved to be well worth everyone's time, as Jeff and Nancy had the opportunity to learn all about the school where Jimmy still serves as principal, and learned more about what all three were passionately working on in their respective jobs to impact student and teacher performance. The personal and professional conversations they had that morning were powerful—so much so that Jimmy and Jeff are in contact almost daily at this point, meeting up online, at national conferences, at local Edcamps, and even at social events. That chance meeting, arranged by a fellow PLN connection, initiated not only a strong personal and professional bond likely to last and grow for the rest of our lives, but also the process that resulted in the book you are reading now.

Of course, when Jeff met Jimmy that day, he immediately began talking to him about Todd, someone who Jimmy knew of and had heard speak on several occasions, but did not know personally. A month later, Jimmy sent a tweet to Jeff with a picture of him having dinner with Todd at a National Association of Secondary School Principals (NASSP) event, tweeting, "I finally met up with your friend @ToddWhitaker." A month after that, Jeff asked Todd to come work with his school teachers and leaders for a day. This time, it was Jeff who insisted Todd come out early the day before so the three could have dinner together. That evening—just over a year ago from the time we began writing this chapter—set in motion more firmly what would become the basis for this book; the excitement for our work, the respect and affection we have for each other, and the way in which we came to share this bond served as but a single example of what we were—and are—seeing happening with thousands of other educators around the world. The power of connecting personally and professionally with educators around the world has changed our lives and made us better at what we do. We hope that by sharing our stories within these pages and, more importantly, connecting readers with the stories of others, we can both empower and inspire other educators to feel the same.

▶ SITUATIONAL CONNECTEDNESS

The concept of "situational leadership" has existed for decades, popularized by leadership experts including Hersey and Blanchard (1985). The theory of situational leadership states that instead of using just one style, successful leaders should change their leadership styles based on various factors, including the maturity of the people they are leading and the details of the task. In this theory, leaders should be able to place more or less emphasis on different variables depending on what is needed to get the job done successfully (Hersey, Blanchard, & Johnson, 2007). According to Hersey and Blanchard (1985), there are four primary leadership styles, which they identify as telling, selling, participating, and delegating. We maintain a parallel theory must exist for connected educators and that we must realize "situational connectedness" is every bit as logical as situational leadership. No single type of leadership style works in every instance. Similarly, no single method of connecting works best in every situation.

Although we make a strong case for establishing an overarching vehicle for educators hoping to expand their knowledge and skill sets and improve their practice by connecting, we also suggest that no one vehicle can accomplish everything we hope to as connected educators. For us, Twitter has become what Joe Mazza (@Joe_Mazza) likes to call the "umbrella" (Mazza, 2014) for nearly all we have learned as connected educators, meaning that many resources we have found, many people we have met, and many opportunities we have been afforded in which to share our learning have come as a result of our presence on Twitter. So, we strongly suggest that other educators do the same. If you have not already "planted that tree," plant it today by getting started on Twitter and connecting with other educators around the world. At the same time, we found that we continue to connect in a variety of other ways, many of which may seem like "old school" methods to some. As proponents of situational connectedness, however, we have found that we continue to grow and learn by connecting with other educators through email, by picking up the phone and calling someone to talk, by taking time to compose handwritten notes, and—perhaps most importantly—by intentionally finding time and opportunities to meet face to face with people as often as possible. The situation we face dictates the type of connection we make, and we never want to lose sight of the importance of connecting with colleagues in person. The tools available to us now make it possible and relatively simple to connect virtually with people around the world. We view this as a tremendous technological breakthrough which allows things to happen that simply could not happen any other way, such as classrooms that can now connect via Skype with other classrooms thousands of miles away, or educators in Canada convening impromptu Google Hangout meetings with educators in Mexico to discuss an issue of mutual interest. Sometimes, the only way we are able to connect with someone is through some electronic format.

At the same time, we found that the relationships we have established initially via Twitter have become even stronger when we subsequently had the opportunity to speak with the person face to face. Interacting with colleagues via Twitter can be extremely beneficial and enjoyable—and even mildly addicting! We exhort others to not fall into the trap of letting their connectedness as educators start and end with Twitter or any other online platform. Take the situation into account to determine what the best way to connect will be.

▶ START NOW: FIRST, WHY? THEN, WHAT?, AND HOW?

Simon Sinek has written and presented extensively about the importance of "starting with why," suggesting in his popular TED Talk that, "People do not buy your what; they buy your why" (Sinek, 2013). Sinek (2013) maintains that "it does not matter *what* we do; it matters *why* we do it." We must first determine why we are engaged in doing whatever it is we do. Then and only then should we move forward and determine what we will actually do and how we will go about doing it. This is good advice for educators who are already intentionally connected or are just now considering what it means to serve as a connected educator. We encourage you to, as Sinek (2011) suggests, start with Why: Why do we become connected educators? Not many—if any—educators we know who have successfully become recognized as leaders in the area of getting connected started down this path just for fun, or to become famous, or to bring attention to themselves, or to follow what Hollywood celebrities are up to, or simply to meet new people. Instead, they have done so, primarily, as a way to grow and improve professionally.

Before committing to becoming a connected educator, ask yourself why you are doing so. Our guess is that if you keep this "why" in mind, the "what" and the "how" will follow naturally, and you will be richly rewarded by making this investment in your personal and professional growth. On the same Twitter chat we referenced above, participants were also asked to share their answers to why they strive to be connected educators. Again, we found many of the answers to be helpful and aligned with our own reasons for connecting with others. Here are just a few:

- John Fritzky @JohnFritzky: The more connected we become the more we can help others learn and learn from others. When that happens #studentswin.
- Ryan Simmelink @MrSimmelink: Helps expand PD (Professional Development) beyond our traditional walls. Experts are willing to share ideas easier. Also allows more personalized PD.
- Deb Day @mrsday75: I am constantly reflecting on what I do when I connect w/others. Always thinking how can I bring these ideas to my room.

- Tammy Stephens @tstephens: Drives excitement energy and enthusiasm for learning.
- Deb Day @mrsday75: I can also model for my kids how to use SM responsibly and to learn. They follow me and can see how I use Twitter.
- Brad Gustafson @GustafsonBrad: Being connected translates into unceasing collaboration for kids. We won't resign to what we think we know within four walls.
- Jennielle Strother @EMjennielle: Experts in their fields have helped shape my opinions on topics beyond what I could imagine through SM (Social Media). Keeps me on my toes.
- John Fritzky @JohnFritzky: It is important to be connected because the work we do as educators is too IMPORTANT to not have access to the best minds.
- Jennifer Houlette @JenHoulette: It's important because you can never be satisfied with staying where you are—there's always more to learn & ways to grow.
- Brianne Koletsos @B_KOL: You can't do it alone. And why would you want to?
- Nathan Lang, EdD @nalang1: Future of education and our world depend on it!

Connected educators, like those in this small sample, are crystal clear about why they strive to connect. In essence, it is about how they can be better, and how they can better serve their students as a result. We found that more and more of our very best educators are working hard to connect with others in an effort to become even more outstanding. If you are currently well along your journey as a connected educator, we applaud you; if you are still waiting to make the leap, we hope you will join us so we can learn with you!

▶ WHO THIS BOOK IS FOR AND HOW TO USE IT

This book is about what connected educators do that sets them apart. Throughout this book we share our own stories, as well as the stories of many other educators we have come to know and respect by being connected to them. We look at where these great connected educators focus their attention, how they spend their time and energy, what guides their decisions, and more importantly how we can learn from them so we can grow and improve, both personally and professionally.

We wrote this book for a wide audience of educators—educators at any grade level from pre-K to higher education. We also wrote this book for educators serving in any role, from school principals, to high school teachers, to university professors, to school superintendents, to librarians, to elementary and middle school teachers. Although connected educators vary widely in geographic locations, job titles, personal traits, and many other factors, what connected educators have in common is also revealing: a zest for lifelong learning, a need to share what they know and learn what others know, a desire to associate with other educators who are equally energized about our noble profession, and a willingness to change and take risks. We found that these traits are shared by those connected educators regardless of what role they currently serve. The roles in which they serve may be vastly diverse; however, the actions they take and the attitudes they hold are what truly set them apart.

The format of this book is straightforward. We hope this introductory chapter provides context on the importance and power of connecting with others who share our passion for all things relating to teaching, learning, and leadership. The following eight chapters each focus on a single action step that connected educators intentionally take to learn and grow. A concluding chapter attempts to connect these eight actions into a composite picture of what it looks like to serve as a connected educator and how we can use this information to transform our classrooms and schools into better places in which to teach and learn.

At the time we were typing this chapter, we noticed that, collectively, we had tweeted out 56,349 messages of no more than 140 characters in length. We suspect that about 95% of those tweets were directly related to educational issues. We also noted that we collectively follow 14,630 other folks on Twitter and are followed by a total of 48,807. Again, we would guess that of these thousands of people whom we follow and count as followers, probably 95% or more are involved in some aspect of education. At times, we drew on the power of this vast PLN in the chapters that follow to illustrate our messages. The bulk of this book consists of the eight items we discovered that connected educators do differently. These eight variables—which we call Key Connectors—are introduced at the outset of each chapter. We provide our own insights as well as examples from many in our PLN. We make a case for why doing each of these eight things not only makes you better at what you do, but also how doing these things will transform the way you look at education overall. From an organizational standpoint, we close each of the eight Key Connectors chapters with three short sections to tie it all together:

1. *Follow 5:* For each Key Connector, we list five educators from our PLN who we believe stand as models in the particular area written about in that chapter. We share a short piece of advice from each of these five educators related to the main topic of the chapter.
2. *Find 5:* For each Key Connector, we share five online resources/tools you can use to further develop yourself in that particular area. These are links to resources that we have learned about via our PLN and that we have used ourselves to improve some aspect of our job performance.
3. *Take 5:* We conclude each chapter by suggesting five action steps you can take to get started or continue as a connected educator.

Thank you for joining us in our own quest to continuously improve and grow by connecting with others. Whether you are just beginning your journey or simply continuing to "plant the trees" of connectedness, we hope you keep us posted on how you are growing as a result!

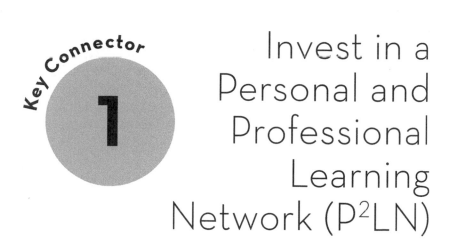

Invest in a Personal and Professional Learning Network (P²LN)

The best minute I spend is the one I invest in people.
Kenneth Blanchard

The jubilation that she had felt during the welcome back to school week had worn off. Gone was the energy of connecting with new faces and interacting with her peers and preparing for the arrival of students who were eager to get back to school after a long summer. She was now alone, in her classroom, removed from the rest of her peers. She was feeling isolated, less effective, and thirsting for some adult personal and professional interaction.
(Graziano, 2005, para. 6)

The scenario described above is all too common in our profession, especially for new teachers who have not had the benefit of establishing a community of support. According to a recent article (Graziano, 2005), nearly half of all new teachers leave the profession within five years. Schools hire more than 200,000 new teachers every year and by the end of the first year, at least 22,000 quit (Graziano, 2005). Moreover, the research shows that of those who do make it beyond year one, 45% leave by the end of their fifth year.

Teaching has often been described as a lonely profession. In many schools, teachers walk into a classroom 180 days each year, shut their door, and do the best they can. They spend 90%

> 66 Educators, like any other professionals, need peer-to-peer interactions and reciprocal investments in order to grow and develop. 99

of their day every day with students, deprived of any significant adult interaction. Over time, this lack of connectivity with other professionals like themselves leads to low efficacy, less risk-taking, low performance, burnout, and high turnover. Sadly, we begin to question whether we can even make a difference. Educators, like any other professionals, need peer-to-peer interactions and reciprocal investments in order to grow and develop. Why is this so critical? Because effective educators recognize the importance and value of making the time to connect with others both personally and professionally in order to avoid these islands of isolation. They know that students who feel connected to a school are more likely to succeed and realize that the same holds true for them as professionals.

It was our intention to include the word "invest" as part of the heading of this chapter. Ultimately, we recognized that the success and impact of any personal learning network depends on the investment of time and effort that each individual is willing to commit not only to others, but to themselves as well. Creating a personal learning network is a collective effort, but unless each of us is willing to give of ourselves, the likelihood of that investment paying off any amount of positive dividends is dubious. Let us be clear: giving of ourselves does not only imply that we are restricted to giving to others, but, equally important, taking time to pause so that we benefit from our own reflection on what we receive in return. These "returns," or fundamental learnings, are part of building and investing in a personal and professional learning network. As we explained in our introduction, Getting Connected, this is often referred to as a "PLN," with the "P" sometimes representing "Personal" and sometimes representing "Professional." We believe that both are equally important and think about this as "P to the Power of 2," or as we sometimes like to call it—a P^2LN, so that, collectively, we continue to grow not only personally, but also professionally, in our learning network.

▶ INVESTING WITH A PURPOSE

Connected educators do not invest in others with the goal of getting something in return. That would be selfish. On the contrary, we aim to encourage others to approach it first from a service mindset, knowing that the key to growing a personal learning network begins and ends with a genuine and sincere effort to connect in order to serve a cause greater than ourselves. In other words, we must be prepared to give of ourselves when we are called to action. We can attest to this point from personal experience as shared below by a member of our P²LN.

> What this author and member of my P²LN taught me in a 10-minute conversation about servant leadership is an experience that I draw from on a regular basis.
>
> I blew it. I had a golden opportunity to earn an assistant principal position in a strong school district, with high academic standards. There was no internal candidate in the running. But, I was also running on empty and I'd been interviewing all week in other places. So, what did I do? I let my emotions get the best of me. You make me wait an additional 45 minutes past my interview time in a room with no air conditioning after I hauled butt to get down there? No apology or reason given when I do get in the room? Is this where I want to be right now? No. And I let them know it through my verbal and nonverbal communication. I wasted my opportunity.
>
> But my P²LN friend wouldn't let me do that. I had another interview the following week. My P²LN colleague believed in me, regardless of the rejections I'd received after previous interviews. I sent him a direct message on Twitter and asked him to call me. He did, from San Antonio, Texas. He was at a conference. I would later learn he was presenting there. I needed a support system and the most important thing for him in that moment was to support me. He invested in me during that conversation; it wasn't so much what he said, but what he did. He called; he listened. And I'll never forget that as I explained how I felt and used an analogy, he replied, "You taught me something." I went out the next day and killed it. I didn't get the position. It went internal. But, I owned that room. The principal called me the following week to tell me how well I did. And, when I'm supporting someone who is struggling through something, I make sure to find a moment to tell them that they taught me something, too.

Today, this person has become an integral part of our P²LN after first connecting somewhat by chance via Twitter. In fact, we made it a point to meet face to face, and we were fortunate to be able to do so a few months later. For fear of sounding over-dramatic, it was close to being a life-changing moment in the sense it brought us even closer together. There is no better feeling than watching someone you connect with grow and develop a sense of confidence that pushes them to be better than they ever thought they could be. Truthfully, investing in others is hard work. It takes energy, time, effort, patience, and a sincere commitment and understanding on our part to recognize that it is not about us, but about what we are able to do for others at any given time. We must be present and intentional with our time so we do not miss opportunities to impact others when they most need our support. Although their goal is not to receive any reward for investing in others, inevitably, connected educators gain as much as they give when they commit to investing in others. These rewards are out there for educators everywhere to reap as soon as we make the conscious decision to take a risk and invest in others. Connected educators know that it all starts with building their own personal *and* professional learning network.

▶ THE POWER OF TWITTER

As connected educators, it is not uncommon for us to be engaged in a conversation with other educators in which the topic of Twitter comes up. With educators not connected professionally on Twitter, this often elicits comments like, "I don't get it," "What is it for?" or "I don't care what Ashton Kutcher or Justin Bieber have to say." We hear stories of how people opened up Twitter accounts, did not see the purpose, and soon after lost interest altogether and gave up on it as a professional learning vehicle. But for many other educators who manage to stay the course, Twitter becomes their "go to" tool for connectivity. In essence, they discovered the power of Twitter, stuck with it, and over time began to see the value and understand the impact that Twitter could eventually have on their own personal and professional growth. So what was the tipping point for these Twitter users? How were they able to do what so many others were unable to do? How were they able to take control of their own learning and begin to cultivate, maintain, and grow a P²LN that made them different from other educators?

▶ GROWING A P²LN THROUGH TWITTER

In order to begin to grow your network through Twitter, it is important that you understand the purpose of your profile. Begin by choosing a Twitter name; we strongly urge you to choose your actual name or something that is very close to your actual name. All Twitter names begin with the @ symbol, so we suggest trying @JohnSmith for your Twitter name (that is, of course, only if your name is "John Smith"). Your goal is not to hide who you are or be clever with your name; instead, you are promoting who you are and what you are interested in professionally in the hope you can connect with other "real" people looking for similar support. The next step is selecting a photograph that best represents you. Once again, it is important to understand you do not want to hide who you are, including what you look like. If you want others to take you seriously, you need to stop being a Twitter "egghead." Users who do not upload a photo of some sort to their profile have, by default, an egg-like image representing themselves instead. Trust us on this: you will not gain a loyal following of learning network members as long as you are a Twitter "egghead"! Connected educators, on the other hand, are anxious to show the world who they are, confident in their professional profile and hoping to connect with other educators who are equally willing to show the world who they are. Educators who grow a strong network on Twitter know it is important to show their face to the world. In addition to a profile picture, Twitter users can add a header, or background picture, which allows you to get creative and share an image that showcases your school, your students, your family, your organization, or anything else you choose to project the professional image you want to share with the world. Almost anything goes when it comes to your header. Have some fun with it.

The next step in creating an effective Twitter profile is to create a short biography. This may be the most important component of your Twitter profile. This is the place to share your story, to tell the world who you are, where you are from, and what you stand for. It is also the place to share a link in order to connect your followers to your blog, Facebook page, or website so they can learn more about you and your personal and professional interests.

Once you establish your profile, it is time to begin building your network. There are many ways to begin the critically important step of learning who to follow and getting others to follow you back. Understand that everyone has something to share that others find profound or valuable. It is imperative that you begin to shift your mindset beyond negative thoughts of "Why would anyone care what I have to say?" and begin to take pride in the fact that you do have unique talents and experiences, and others not only can, but will, learn from you. Use the search key to find other educators who are active on Twitter and begin to view their lists of who they follow as suggested resources. Do not feel strange about reading their bios, viewing their tweets, and scrutinizing their list of who they follow and who follows them. This is how we all get started growing our learning network. Your purpose is to grow a network of professional colleagues with whom you can interact: conversing, gathering information, learning from, sharing your own ideas, and exchanging resources. Tweet to others using their Twitter name, which always begins with the @ symbol, and ask specific questions. However, do not feel as though you have to tweet constantly. Start slow. We recommend starting with, perhaps, something as simple as four tweets a day: ask a question, share a resource, respond to a comment tweeted out by someone else, and, lastly, tweet out something personal that speaks to who you are. Eventually, this can create your personal niche with others connected on Twitter. Also, it is perfectly acceptable to "lurk" (a term used for simply following the Twitter stream and not tweeting back in return). You can learn a lot merely by watching all the amazing resources and ideas shared by others. As your network grows and your comfort level of being connected improves, you may catch yourself not wanting to miss the flow of tweets. This may happen. If so, keep perspective that it is

> **❝**It is imperative that you begin to shift your mindset beyond negative thoughts of 'Why would anyone care what I have to say?' and begin to take pride in the fact that you do have unique talents and experiences.**❞**

called a Twitter stream for a reason. Just a like a stream of water, your Twitter stream will flow all day and night and that is okay. When you are ready to dive back in, you can just pick up where you left off. There will always be a new flow of tweets ready for you to view, mark as favorite, and/or retweet.

There is no timeline or mandatory minimum regarding when and how often you should begin tweeting. Go at your own pace, but do not let fear drive your timeline, rather embrace your vulnerability. Once you begin to interact with others via Twitter, you slowly see your confidence rise and your number of followers begin to increase. Be prepared to eventually hit a plateau of followers. It will happen until you are ready to expand your participation. Do not let this deter you. Keep at it. Push yourself to take risks and take part in a chat (this is discussed in greater detail in Chapter 2). Taking part in Twitter chats will expand your audience and allow you to interact with others who share a similar interest in a specific topic. By doing so, you will continue to increase the number of people with similar interests you follow as well as gain your own additional followers; in other words, you will begin to firmly establish your P²LN!

On occasion, we hear others share how they do not want any followers or they do not care about their number of followers. Well, they should and so should you. Not because connecting via Twitter is a popularity contest or having a large following is some sort of status symbol, but because in order to make the greatest possible impact you can, you will want the greatest audience possible with whom to connect. This is one way that connected educators think differently. As we discuss in Chapter 4, they want to give, take, and then give some more to as many people as possible. By doing so, they begin to grow and expand their network to a global scale. Some educators we know are comfortable doing what they have always done and learning only from people with whom they interact at their own school. Connected educators strive for more; they feel obliged to expand their professional learning network in order to become better at what they do and, ultimately, better meet the needs of the students and/or colleagues they serve.

By connecting with other educators on Twitter, you have access to a plethora of resources and a host of other educators eager to learn and share their knowledge with you. Our

> **"**Your presence on the 'Twitterverse' gives you the opportunity to expand your knowledge, which leads to more opportunities to teach others what you have learned and allow you to make an even greater impact on others than you ever thought possible.**"**

experience, not unlike many of our networked colleagues, has been that participating in the educational community via Twitter has rekindled a strong sense of renewal to our profession. We urge you to join the growing legion of connected educators on Twitter—not only will you learn from others, but you can also contribute by giving back of your time and resources, which in turn helps our profession as a whole. Your presence on the "Twitterverse" gives you the opportunity to expand your knowledge, which leads to more opportunities to teach others what you have learned and allow you to make an even greater impact on others than you ever thought possible. Moreover, getting connected inspires you to expand your circle of professional colleagues outside your own organization to include others around the world who also desire to develop meaningful professional relationships in an effort to better serve their students, parents, and colleagues. In short, you become encouraged and professionally challenged to strive for greatness!

▶ MAKING, NOT MARKING, TIME

For years, educators everywhere have lived their professional lives on islands of isolation. Our roles as educators are somewhat of a paradox—we are surrounded daily by scores of students and colleagues and have hundreds of personal interactions a day, yet we often find ourselves feeling alone. From a professional standpoint, our days and evenings can be spent on lesson preparation, searching online resources, collecting materials, responding to emails, interacting with students, providing feedback on homework assignments, or completing the multitude of other daily tasks our work requires us to do. However, much of what we do is still spent working independently or on individual tasks that do not require much meaningful adult interaction. How often have you heard colleagues share that they sometimes go an entire work day and feel like they never left their classroom or their office? Or how often do you hear staff members talk about how they sometimes go days or even weeks without seeing some of their own colleagues? Sound familiar?

The truth is this is an all-too-common experience for thousands of educators around the world. Yet, we elect to continue on with our daily lives like we are living in some prison of unfulfilled connectivity.

For educators feeling unfulfilled in their professional lives, we have three words of advice: Get Connected Today! Getting connected both professionally and personally can be a life-changing event for educators. Yet, the notion of expanding our networks beyond the traditional means of email, telephone calls, educational workshops, and conferences can be an overwhelming process for many educators new to the possibilities that web-based technologies can offer them. After all, we can barely manage the work we have now; we certainly do not have time to keep up with the constant changes in technology and the information overflow that comes with tools such as Twitter, Facebook, Instagram, Pinterest, Google Plus, Skype, Google Hangouts, and Voxer—just to name a few. Or do we? The fact is we must *make* the time. The global society in which we live has changed dramatically in the past few decades and we must be prepared to model for our students and for our colleagues a willingness to embrace this change.

We can begin by connecting with others around the globe. It is hard to believe that the Internet—something we now take for granted—is a relatively recent phenomenon. In fact, it was not until April 1993 that the World Wide Web technology became available for anyone to use on a royalty-free basis. "Since that time, however, the Web has changed the world. It has arguably become the most powerful communication medium the world has ever known" (World Wide Web Foundation, 2014, para. 5).

The time has come for all educators to fully embrace the opportunities this amazing resource offers us—and our students. Scott McLeod, Founding Director of the UCEA Center for the Advanced Study of Technology Leadership in Education (CASTLE), makes the case for educators to once and for all embrace 21st-century teaching and learning, suggesting that embracing this shift in mindset begins with making the conscious decision to become a connected educator (McLeod, 2011). McLeod challenges us with important questions about what we must do in our schools and classrooms. Make no mistake about it: these are big questions. Answering confidently requires us to band together and become connected. The answer lies within the personal, professional networks we create, maintain, and grow:

- When are we going to start integrating technology into our schooling lives like we do in our personal lives and in our non-school professional lives? In other words, when will we stop pretending it is a notebook-paper and ring-binder world out there?
- What percentage of our school technology budget goes toward teacher-centric technologies (e.g., interactive whiteboards) rather than student-centric technologies (e.g., laptops)?
- Our kids live in a world in which they expect to be able to create, publish, share, collaborate, connect, and have a voice. What can we do to tap into the educational power of our students as online collaborators, creators, sharers, and contributors?
- How are we (or should we be) tapping into the power of technology to facilitate differentiated, individualized, personalized learning experiences for our students?
- Schools typically move at incremental, linear rates of change. But everything around us is moving at an exponential, revolutionary rate of change. It is like the Industrial Revolution crammed into 15 years instead of 150. Are we facilitating linear or exponential change in our school organization?
- In all of our efforts to teach students safe, appropriate, and responsible technology use, are we forgetting the more important job of teaching our students empowered use?
- Everything is moving to the Web. Everything. When we teach our students how to write, are we teaching our students how to do so in hyperlinked, networked, interconnected online spaces for authentic, relevant worldwide audiences?
- Do we really understand what our kids are doing with social media or is what we know primarily from the news media?
- Are we intentionally, purposefully, and explicitly modeling these new technology literacies for our students?

- Do we truly "get it"? Are we doing what really needs to be done to prepare students for a hyper-competitive global information economy and for the demands of digital, global citizens? (McLeod, 2011, paras A, C, D, E, F, G, H, I, L, O)

Effectively answering these questions requires us to band together and learn from each other. We often hear the term "lifelong learner" being overused in educational organizations to the point that it is at risk of becoming yet another educational cliché. Connected educators, on the other hand, see this as their mission: to not only serve as lifelong learners, but also to model lifelong learning for their students. They know they cannot learn it all on their own, so they work intentionally to establish a network of fellow lifelong learners. Over time, these professional networks have evolved into incredible personal relationships as well. The opportunity to spend quality time and engage in meaningful dialogue with other educators who also aspire to be better eventually becomes a primary goal of connected educators. These personal connections allow us to set our own barometer for how, with whom, and when we want to connect. In the past, these connections were somewhat more limited, their number often restricted to lack of accessibility due to location, time, or other factors. Today, these factors have become nearly obsolete with the introduction of virtual tools which allow us to engage in wide open spaces and extend our learning opportunities to unlimited boundaries.

We have a tremendous opportunity within our grasp to make not only a professional impact on others, but a personal one as well. What we expect of ourselves is what we get in return. If we want to prepare our students for the rest of this century and beyond, then we must quit living in the last half century and recognize the value of becoming not only a connected educator, but also a connected, lifelong learner. The more we consciously strive to serve as connected educators, the more likely it is we can support our students in becoming connected learners.

▶ FINDING VALUE IN LEARNING NETWORKS

Math students are often asked to give their answer in "simplest terms," causing them to struggle to find the right solution to a problem. What they fail to recognize is that sometimes you have to change the equation in order to find the exact value you are looking for. The same can be said about learning networks. Recently, we overheard one educator saying to another, "Some days it feels like I am all alone running on a treadmill and I don't feel like I am going anywhere." This person is not alone in feeling this way, but like other educators who feel this way, she must realize that perhaps it is time to change the equation. Rather than run alone on a treadmill, this individual could benefit from joining a Sunday morning running group. If you have ever joined a running group then you know what it feels like to join a group of passionate individuals with similar interests who share a common goal, right? Simply put, it jacks you up! Well, the same feeling exists when you join a learning network of educators who are committed to making a difference for all kids and who aspire to be excellent. Angela Maiers (@AngelaMaiers), an educator, author, and speaker who is passionate about the use of social media and its impact on our world, says that "Every person wants to matter. Everyone wants to do work that matters. Secure their heart and their passion and you will be inspired by their contribution."

If you have ever heard Angela speak you know she means what she says and she says what she means. Angela has modeled what it means to be connected and has found value in her learning network by connecting with educators worldwide to spread her message to learners of all ages of the power of reading, writing, and global communication. Like Angela, there are educators all across America who have found the value of becoming a connected learner and joining a network of passionate educators all interested in what they can do to make a difference.

Brad Currie (@bcurrie5), a New Jersey school administrator and co-founder/moderator of one of the more popular educational chats on Twitter (#satchat), is a perfect example of what one person's commitment to becoming a connected educator has meant for not only his own growth as a professional, but how he has been able to leverage his learning to transform his school. Currie's (2014) post entitled "Take Action" describes in detail specific changes that have come about at his school, Black River Middle School. In other words, the value he has gained from his learning network served as the catalyst for many of the changes at his school that came about as a result of his learning and inspiration from others to whom he is connected. His post can be viewed here at http://www.bradcurrie.net/blog/taking-action.

Educators around the globe are transforming their classrooms and schools by stepping outside their comfort zones, finding value in their connectivity, and utilizing free tools accessible to them via their computer, iPad, and smartphones which allow them to connect with like-minded colleagues on a daily basis. They are forming "connected communities," which, in turn, is elevating them to greater heights and ultimately benefitting their school communities and students in positive ways.

Our profession has been silent and isolated for too long. We have paddled our way through this vast sea we call teaching and learning on our own for way too long. The time is now for us to take responsibility for owning our professional learning by networking with individuals who share our passion and our desire to be the change! In order to do so, however, we must find the time to consistently "take that one minute" to invest in other people as well as ourselves. Only then will we have the opportunity to reach our full potential as professional educators. Connected educators start along the path of connectivity by investing in a personal and professional learning network. Every subsequent step along this journey happens as a result of modeling the way and taking this initial step.

> 66 We have paddled our way through this vast sea we call teaching and learning on our own for way too long. The time is now for us to take responsibility for owning our professional learning by networking with individuals who share our passion and our desire to be the change! 99

FOLLOW 5, FIND 5, TAKE 5

For additional insights into establishing a P²LN and making it work to enhance your life as a connected educator, we suggest you **Follow 5** educators who are leaders in investing in their own learning networks, **Find 5** resources we have shared, which helps you to create and maintain your own learning network, and **Take 5** specific action steps which set the wheels in motion for becoming a connected educator.

Follow 5: These five educators from our learning network stand as models in the area of investing in a P²LN, which we have written about in this chapter. We have listed their names and Twitter "handles." We encourage you to follow these exemplary educators on Twitter and interact with them to enhance your life as a connected educator. Here are short pieces of advice from these experts in the field on investing in a personal and professional learning network:

1. *Joe Sanfelippo (@joesanfelippofc)*. Superintendent of Fall Creek, Wisconsin School District. Co-host of @BrandEDPodcast. Joe regularly participates in #wischat. According to Sanfelippo, "My PLN is essentially like being in the best staff lounge ever. People share, connect, and help each other personally and professionally. It allows me to model continuous learning for our staff and students."

2. *Cristina Zimmerman (@CristinaZimmer4)*. Spanish teacher at Bettendorf High School in Bettendorf, Iowa. Cristina regularly participates in #IAedchat, #langchat, #edtechchat. According to Zimmerman,

Using Twitter can be an overwhelming experience for some educators, but the time investment in learning how it works pays huge dividends. There is no better platform for networking with other teachers. For those educators who struggle with the hashtags and symbols, I suggest that they get started using Pinterest or Facebook as a means of professional development; however, the real learning takes place when you have a place to exchange ideas with other teachers and this is what Twitter does best.

3. *William M Ferriter (@plugusin)*. Sixth grade classroom teacher in Raleigh, North Carolina. According to Ferriter,

Investing in a professional learning network can help any classroom teacher gain ready access to materials that they can use in their classrooms immediately. My lessons are almost always influenced by the content shared by the people that I follow. More importantly, however, investing in a professional learning network can help any classroom teacher gain ready access to like-minded peers that can leave them energized and inspired. The colleagues that I've connected with are a source of constant real-time support and instant smiles that I turn to whenever I'm feeling discouraged or overwhelmed. They are a reminder that I'm NOT alone. #thatmatters

4. *Todd Nesloney (@techninjatodd)*. Principal of Navasota Intermediate in Navasota, Texas. Co-host of @EduAllstarsHQ. According to Nesloney,

My PLN has provided me with a set of individuals who continually challenge me, push me further, and provide a listening ear. I know for a fact I would not be the individual in education that I am today, without the influence of my PLN. I always say, "You are who you surround yourself with," and I believe that I surround myself with the best people in the world through my learning network.

5. *Jenna Shaw (@teachbaltshaw)*. Middle school language arts teacher in Baltimore, Maryland. Jenna regularly participates in #edtech-chat and #IAedchat. According to Shaw,

We live in an amazingly large world that is full of extremely wise people, yet on a daily basis we only get to interact with a tiny portion of the population and tap into a droplet of that wisdom. Building a community of learners through a PLN has helped me gain strength, courage, knowledge, and compassion through expanding my reach and relationships outside my school community, stretching into a global space of learning and growing. Through these connections I have gained thought-partners, critical friends, and true companions that push me to be a better person in all areas of my life.

Find 5: We have found these five online resources/tools to be particularly useful in getting started building your P²LN. These are links to resources that we have learned about via our PLN and that we have used ourselves to improve some aspect of our job performance:

1. Twitter in 60 Seconds: https://www.youtube.com/watch?v=ZYz9M70KVR0.
2. Twitter tutorial by @stumpteacher: http://stumpteacher.blogspot.com/2010/12/twitter-tutorial.html.
3. Hashtags in 60 Seconds: https://www.youtube.com/watch?v=cD0dT81ChIU.
4. Top 10 Ways to Get More Followers on Twitter: http://computer.howstuffworks.com/internet/social-networking/information/10-ways-to-get-more-followers-on-twitter.htm#page=1.
5. Growing Your PLN with Twitter: http://plpnetwork.com/2012/04/20/growing-your-pln-with-twitter-2/.

Take 5: We conclude each chapter by recommending five action steps you can take to get started or continue as a connected educator. Here are five steps we suggest you take to get started in growing your PLN:

1. Open up a Twitter account and create a professional profile and brief biography.
2. Research one connected educator a day for ten days via Twitter. Observe not only their profile, but also what they tweet, how often they tweet, who they follow, who follows them, and in which Twitter chats they participate.
3. Follow at least 50 educators who "speak" to you within the first month of opening your account.
4. Send out at least four tweets each day during your first week on Twitter: ask a question, share a resource, respond to a comment tweeted out by someone else, and, last, tweet out something personal that speaks to who you are.
5. Set a goal to gain 50 followers in the first month of opening your Twitter account.

Learn What They Want, When They Want, How They Want

You can't teach people everything they need to know.
The best you can do is position them where they can find
what they need to know when they need to know it.

Seymour Papert

Connected educators love learning. They do not necessarily limit their love of professional learning to traditional delivery models—at least not for all of their professional learning needs. Instead, they find ways to learn from other educators any time, anywhere, and by any means that best suit their learning goals. Much has been written in recent years about a move toward personalizing learning for *students* (Clarke, 2003; Freedman, 2009; Gardner, 2010; Schneiderman, 2010). Yet much less has been written about personalized learning for *educators* (Freedman, 2009). However, connected educators around the world have taken matters into their own hands and begun "personalizing" their learning by reaching out to colleagues near and far in an effort to learn as much as possible about how to continuously get better at what they do. Connected educators have found that the best people from whom to learn are, quite simply, other educators who are facing similar issues and are similarly seeking new ideas and new solutions for the challenges they face. As but one example of the need and desire to learn from job-alike colleagues, an art teacher teaching in a school at which she is the sole art teacher may well find some professional learning events offered at the school or district helpful to what she is doing in her classroom; however, much of what an art teacher needs to learn to get better and grow can only be obtained by collaborating with other art teachers. By connecting with other art teachers around the world, she is able to personalize her own learning, getting what she really wants and needs to know in order to improve as an art teacher. Connected educators find ways to connect with others who share their learning interests so they can learn **what** they want to learn.

> **"**Many find that learning outside the scope of the school day provides them not only the flexibility they desire, but also a more comfortable, relaxed environment for learning.**"**

Connected educators—like almost all educators—are extremely busy and cannot always maximize their own learning opportunities during the course of "regular" school business hours. Instead, many find that learning outside the scope of the school day provides them not only the flexibility they desire, but also a more comfortable, relaxed environment for learning. At many schools in which we have worked, we find that dedicated professional learning hours are few and far between. If you are teaching in a typical public school today, chances are slim that you spend even an hour a week learning something new about your practice that is embedded into your school work schedule. Sadly, there is simply not enough time during work-week hours for connected educators to learn all that they need and want to learn. Moreover, oftentimes our days are so action-packed that by the end of the school day, all we want to do is go home and relax for a while. Attending workshops of an hour or more at the close of a busy school day is not always the best time to learn new ideas for becoming better at what we do. As a result, connected educators have begun finding time in the evening hours and even on weekends to learn and grow professionally; they seek out and find opportunities to learn **when** they choose to.

In the past decade, connected educators have begun learning what and when they want, not limiting themselves to the learning topics offered through their school districts or the hours for which they are contractually obliged to be present. They are actively engaged in "anytime" learning about topics they find personally and professionally relevant. In addition to connecting with others when they want about what they want, connected educators also determine **how** they learn best and intentionally plan to learn in the ways that suit their learning styles. We have already suggested that Twitter is the "how" for many connected educators with whom we have worked. The use of Twitter as a professional learning resource for educators is a refrain throughout this book. In this chapter, we look at certain aspects of Twitter that are ideal for educators wishing to learn **what** they want, **when** they want, and **how** they want.

▶ TWITTER HASHTAGS

On Twitter, the # sign has become known as a "hashtag." According to Twitter support personnel, "the hashtag is a symbol used to mark key words or topics in a Tweet" (Using hashtags on Twitter, 2014, para. 1). Like so much else about the Twitter community, it was created organically by Twitter users as a way to categorize messages. People use the hashtag symbol before a relevant phrase or keyword in their tweets to categorize them and to connect with others who are interested in the same topic. Connected educators use Twitter hashtags at times to share and find tweets that include references to and/or resources for a topic about which they are trying to learn more. As an example, just now in looking at our Twitter feed, we saw the following tweet from Mike Nitzel (@MikeNitzel), a principal of a K-6 school in Rock Island, Illinois, "10 Awesome Ways to Inspire Others #leadership zite.to/1kSOGl3".

In this tweet, Mike—who, as a school principal, is very interested in leadership—has shared a link to an article about how leaders inspire others, and included a hashtag: #leadership. By including the hashtag, Mike is first and foremost sharing an article that he found worth reading about a topic that is near and dear to his professional learning interests. In addition, he included the #leadership hashtag so that others who see the words of his tweet ("10 Awesome Ways to Inspire Others") will know it is an article about leadership. People who are, like Mike, interested in leadership may well click on the hashtag. When the user clicks on any hashtagged word, it reveals a column of any other tweets that were marked with that hashtag. So by clicking on "#leadership" in Mike's tweet, someone on Twitter can find scores of other comments, ideas, questions, quotes, and links to resources on this topic of interest.

There are hundreds of hashtags commonly used by connected educators. Middle school educators looking to connect with other middle-level educators or find resources relating to middle school may include the #middleschool hashtag in their tweets at times. Science, Technology, Engineering, and Mathematics (STEM) is becoming an increasingly popular focus for educators around the world, so when sending STEM-related tweets, connected educators may choose to include the #STEM hashtag. Similarly, educators passionate about Project Based Learning (#PBL), Social Emotional Learning (#SEL), or mathematics (#math) will, at times, include the appropriate hashtag to focus attention on the topic about which they are tweeting. A very common hashtag found on Twitter and included by users of all career paths is #FF, which stands for "Friday Follow." Every Friday, some Twitter users send out a tweet with the #FF hashtag suggesting people to follow on Twitter. Connected educators use this as a way to recognize colleagues who have been helpful resources to them, knowing that if they find the person a supportive member of their own PLN, others they are connected to may want to follow the person as well.

In addition to sending out tweets with a hashtag relating to a topic of interest included, connected educators can also simply search a topic of interest by typing a hashtag into the search box available on Twitter. For example, after typing the #classroommanagement hashtag into the search box just now, we immediately found a dozen or more resources relating to the topic which looked not only relevant, but also very practical for anyone interested in getting better at this important area of our work. Whether the goal is to share ideas/resources or to get ideas/resources on a topic of interest, using hashtags is a helpful way for connected educators to focus their professional learning when communicating via Twitter.

▶ TWITTER CHATS

One of the single most powerful ways educators connect with others is by participating in Twitter chats. Twitter chats are a pre-arranged online discussion about a specific topic that anyone can join. Typically, Twitter chats for educators occur each week at the same time. A Twitter chat is another way that hashtags are used on Twitter. Each time someone participates in a Twitter chat, they include the hashtag describing the chat (for example, #IAedchat for Iowa Edchat that Jimmy co-founded and co-moderates) at the end of each tweet. The hashtag associates your tweet with the particular Twitter chat and topic. You must have a Twitter account to participate. Many members of our PLN find that using Tweetdeck.com is a helpful platform when participating in a Twitter chat. Every Twitter chat has a moderator—or co-moderators—who hosts the chat. They start by tweeting out reminders up to a week before the chat, letting educators who may be interested know what the topic is on any given week and reminding everyone when the chat will occur. During the actual chat, over the course of an hour the moderator(s) poses a series of questions related to the topic. Typically, a chat poses approximately seven questions spaced out over the hour time block. Educators participating in the chat can then respond to each question and respond to another participant's answer to the question. The Twitter chat forum for exchanging ideas on a specific topic has become an increasingly popular way for educators around the world to engage and connect.

> **"**One of the single most powerful ways educators connect with others is by participating in Twitter chats. Twitter chats are a pre-arranged online discussion about a specific topic that anyone can join.**"**

We strongly encourage you to read the information and resources in the *Follow 5, Find 5, Take 5* section below, where you find links to very helpful Twitter chat resources as well as steps to take for participating in a Twitter chat. Be sure to take a look at the official schedule of educational tweet chats. This document lists over 300 educational chats that occur weekly and is organized by the day of the week on which chats are hosted. We can honestly say that there is a regularly scheduled Twitter chat for you, no matter what your role is in education. Whether you are an elementary school counselor (#escchat: 8:00–9:00 p.m. CST Thursdays), a new teacher (#ntchat: 8:00–9:00 p.m. ET Wednesdays), or a music teacher (#musedchat: 8:00–9:00 p.m. ET Mondays), there is a chat just for you which includes educators who, like you, are passionate about their jobs and interested in connecting with others who are equally passionate about a specific role in education. Chat participants are eager to exchange ideas about how to keep growing and getting better in that particular role.

In addition to very job-specific chats focusing on aspects of a job that would appeal primarily to certain subject area or grade-level teachers, there are many chats that are geared toward general educational topics. Examples include #edchat (twice each Tuesday, 12:00–1:00 p.m. ET and 7:00–8:00 p.m. ET), a Twitter conversation that any educator can join to discuss and learn about current teaching trends, how to integrate technology, transform their teaching, and connect with inspiring educators worldwide. Through #edchat, participants also discuss education policy, education reform, and often have leaders in the field of education from around the world join in the chat. Other examples include the weekly state chats that occur in more than 40 of the 50 United States (for a complete list of state edchats, please see http://www.eschoolnews.com/2014/05/28/state-twitter-chats-438/2/.

Like anything new that one tries, getting started with Twitter chats can be challenging at first. In large chats, sometimes the tweets are coming at you so fast that it may be difficult to figure out how to keep up. Other times, you may find that there are only a few people participating and you may not feel as if you are getting any new ideas. We implore you to stick with it; the more you participate in Twitter chats, the more likely your circle of PLN members will expand, allowing you access to more and more educators sincerely interested in making a difference. Do not be afraid to reach out to your PLN for help: we have found that members of our PLN are always willing to do whatever it takes to help a colleague who is just getting started as a connected educator. Moreover, your persistence will pay off as you begin learning, growing, and connecting through Twitter chats. It is virtually impossible to follow every tweet that is written during the course of a Twitter chat, even if there are a small number of educators participating in a given chat, and to help with this, most chat moderators archive the entire chat (using a tool such as Storify) and share the record of all tweets posted during the entire chat so participants—and others who may have missed the chat—can go back and review what was discussed and shared. Twitter chats are a perfect example of connected educators learning what they want, when they want, and how they want.

> **❝**Twitter chats are a perfect example of connected educators learning what they want, when they want, and how they want.**❞**

▶ EDCAMPS

Although Twitter is an ideal way for us to learn anything, any time, and anywhere, we said at the outset of this book that connected educators do not limit their learning solely to online opportunities. In fact, although Twitter is an extremely effective and efficient professional learning resource, nothing beats learning alongside other connected educators face to face. One such type of "in-person" learning event that has gained a great deal of momentum recently is known as an "Edcamp." An Edcamp is a type of "unconference," a loosely structured conference that emphasizes an informal exchange of information and ideas between participants, rather than following a conventionally structured program of events with keynote speakers and planned sessions led by experts on a topic who have prepared to deliver a formal presentation. In unconferences, such as Edcamps, the learning is driven more by the participants than it is by the organizers.

> **❝** In unconferences, such as Edcamps, the learning is driven more by the participants than it is by the organizers.**❞**

In the past several years, organizers around the world have scheduled hundreds of official Edcamps. The number of official Edcamps has grown from 8 total in 2010, to 51 in 2011, to 125 in 2012, and to 191 in 2013 (Edcamp Foundation, 2014). They have convened around the globe, from Stockholm, Sweden, to Rocky Mountain House, Alberta, Canada, to Cape Girardeau, Missouri (Edcamp Foundation, 2014). In addition, more and more schools and school districts are devoting a portion of their precious professional learning time to hosting informal Edcamps within their own school or district. Edcamps allow all who attend to have an equal voice in what they learn and to what extent they will actively participate in any session they join. Although Edcamps vary widely in terms of locations in which they occur, they are all more alike than different. All Edcamps share the following in common:

- They are free to attend
- They are non-commercial and conducted with a vendor-free presence
- They are hosted by any organization interested in furthering the Edcamp mission
- They are made up of sessions that are determined on the day of the event
- They are events where anyone who attends can be a presenter
- They are reliant on the "law of two feet" that encourages participants to find a session that meets their needs. (Edcamp Foundation, n.d., para. 5)

Edcamps typically begin with a free breakfast of some sort and also include a free lunch for all who attend. They often occur on a Saturday morning and involve approximately two hundred participants. Often, someone from the host site welcomes attendees and then the fun begins: there is a call out to everyone in the audience who wants to see a session offered on any topic to come to the microphone and share what exactly they are hoping to learn more about through an informal dialogue with others in attendance who are also interested in the topic. The person suggesting the session topic does not necessarily "lead" the session, though they may facilitate the conversation. Sessions last for approximately an hour and there tend to be four sessions throughout the day. Although session topics at Edcamps can run the gamut of all possible ideas relating to education, according to Kristen Swanson (@kristenswanson), the topics "aren't merely fluffy concepts. They are specific, practical strategies and ideas that educators are sharing and investigating at Edcamps all over the nation" (Swanson, 2013, para. 11). Swanson (2013) also analyzed the responses Edcamp attendees have written subsequent to attending an Edcamp. She found that the most common themes mentioned by participants were:

- Collaboration and connections
- Group expertise

- Tech tools
- Instructional design
- Surprise (at the number of educators dedicated to their craft). (Edcamp Foundation, 2012, para. 3)

Many educators (including each of the authors of this book) still make it a priority to attend traditional professional conferences held at the local, regional, and national scale. At the same time, an increasing number of connected educators are looking to non-traditional professional learning conferences—or unconferences—to broaden their knowledge base, increase their skill set, and meet like-minded educators with whom they can build lasting professional relationships beyond the conference itself. Professional learning events like Edcamps are another example of connected educators seeking opportunities to learn what they want, when they want, and how they want. At the outset of this chapter, we referenced a quote that wisely points out the futility of trying to teach a person everything there is to know about any topic. This includes ourselves: we simply will never know all there is to learn about education. This reality holds true and is worth noting not only when we decide what, when, and how to teach our students, but also when we are trying to learn ourselves. Connected educators hold this truth as self-evident and, as a result, position themselves to be able to learn: **what** they need to know, **when** they choose to learn it, and **how** they go about gaining the learning they need to grow continuously.

FOLLOW 5, FIND 5, TAKE 5

Follow 5: These five educators from our PLN stand as models in the area of learning any time, anywhere, in the way that works best for them, which we have written about in this chapter. We have listed their names along with their Twitter "handles." We encourage you to follow these exemplary educators on Twitter and interact with them to enhance your life as a connected educator. Here are short insights from these experts in the field on learning what you want, when you want, and how you want:

1. *Tom Murray (@thomascmurray)*. State and District Digital Learning Director, Alliance for Excellent Education, Washington, DC. Tom moderates #edtechchat, which takes place on Mondays from 8:00–9:00 p.m. EST. Tom also regularly participates in #edchat, #IAedchat, #satchat, and #ptchat. According to Murray,

Twitter chats offer an engaging, relevant, differentiated form of professional learning for all involved. These conversations have become an excellent way for educators to connect on relevant topics, share resources and best practices, all while challenging each other's thinking. Twitter chats are a regular component to my own personalized learning plan.

2. *Maria Galanis (@mariagalanis)*. Instructional coach, Deerfield Public Schools District 109. Maria regularly participates in #IAedchat, #iledchat, #satchat, #akedchat, #aledchat, and #educoach. According to Galanis,

Being a connected educator means loving what you do so much that you want to continually become better at it, and grow. One of the most powerful ways for me to do this is by finding a little time, and joining in on weekly Twitter chats. I consider them passion-based learning opportunities, and love the connections with others from all over, near and far, who are interested in the same thing. Being a little vulnerable by sharing your thoughts on a topic, and hearing different points of view, can make you grow exponentially as a person, and as a professional.

3. *Lauren Taylor (@LTaylorELA)*. Eighth grade reading teacher, Kansas City, MO. Lauren moderates #innoed, which takes place on Mondays at 6:00–7:00 p.m. CST. Lauren also regularly participates in #sblchat, #weirded, #engchat, #nbtchat, and #moedchat. According to Taylor,

I believe that it is important for teachers to take control of their own learning. Professional development should allow educators to choose what they want to learn and how they want to learn it, much like how we provide options for our students. Twitter is the perfect platform for that. It grants us access to brilliant educators around the world in order to build a PLN and take part in PD when we choose. I call it "world wisdom at my fingertips."

4. *Dr. Joe Mazza (@joe_mazza)*. University of Pennsylvania's Graduate School of Education instructor, digital strategist, innovation coach. Joe moderates #ptchat, which takes place on Wednesdays at 9:00–10:00 p.m. EST and #pennedchat are a part of the @MCDPEL school leadership efforts. According to Mazza,

For me, today's professional learning has become a lot more personalized than it used to be. By choosing to be connected, every day I have the opportunity to learn from others whom I consider to be not only good people, and educators, but inspirers and thought-provokers around the world in the educational community. I no longer have a need to wait for my local school district or employer to set the table for my own professional learning. The best part about this personal learning movement for educators: it doesn't require approval nor a purchase order on the part of administration.

5. *Daisy Dyer Duerr (@DaisyDyerDuerr)*. Pre-K-12 Principal, Arkansas. Daisy moderates #arkedchat Thursdays, 8:00–9:00 p.m. CST. She also regularly participates in #satchat, #ptchat, and many state Edchats. According to Duerr,

Edchats have provided an amazing forum for educators to share ideas on various topics and even more importantly MAKE CONNECTIONS with each other. Edchats have been instrumental in the building of my Professional/Personal Learning Network. I have taken away many great ideas from my various interactions on Edchats, but even more importantly, I have taken away lifelong connections with AWESOME educators that help me grow as a professional daily!

Find 5: We have found these five online resources/tools to be particularly useful in finding your personal path to professional learning. These are links to resources that we have learned about via our PLN and that we have used ourselves to improve some aspect of our job performance:

1. A Simple Guide on the Use of the Hashtag for Teachers: http://www.educatorstechnology.com/2013/05/a-simple-guide-on-use-of-hashtag-for.html (Educational Technology and Mobile Learning: A resource of educational web tools and mobile apps for teachers and educators, 2013).
2. Popular Education Hashtags on Twitter: http://www.november learning.com/twitterhashtags (November Learning, n.d.).
3. Official Twitter Educational Chat Schedule: https://sites.google.com/site/twittereducationchats/education-chat-calendar (The Weekly Twitter Chat Times, n.d.).
4. The Power of Twitter Chats (this is a link to a video, approximately 30 minutes in length, highlighting several connected educators discussing the use of Twitter chats): https://www.youtube.com/watch?feature=player_embedded&v=brI8sHmg89w (Murray, 2013).
5. Edcamp The Complete Guide: How To Start & Run Your Very Own Edcamp: http://Edcamp.wikispaces.com/file/view/HowTo Edcamp.pdf (Simple K12, n.d.).

Take 5: We conclude each chapter by recommending five action steps you can take to get started or continue as a connected educator. Here are five steps we suggest you take in order to learn what you want, when you want, and how you want:

1. Pick a hashtag from the list in item number 2 in "Find 5" that is relevant to your role in education. Type the hashtag into the search feature of Twitter (or any other Twitter platform you might use, such as Tweetdeck or HootSuite). Note what types of tweets show up in the stream. Click on any resources shared in the stream until you find one that is meaningful to you.

2. Send out a tweet on a Friday asking those who follow you on Twitter to also follow three to five members from your PLN who share worthwhile tweets on a consistent basis in your opinion. Be sure to include the #FF hashtag.

3. If you have not already done so, take part in a Twitter chat. If you are a veteran Twitter chat participant, find one from the list in number 3 in "Find 5" that you have never joined and try it out. After participating, be sure to follow a few educators from the chat whom you met for the first time via the chat.

4. Attend an Edcamp. Go to the official Edcamp Wikispace (http://Edcamp.wikispaces.com/) to see the list of past Edcamps that have been organized around the world and look at ones that are upcoming. Make the commitment to attend one nearby. If you have already attended the ones held annually in your location, make a commitment to attend one further away that you have yet to experience.

5. Try to organize an informal Edcamp in your school or district. Depending on your role, either ask your principal or district administrator if they would be willing to set aside some professional development time to try this. If you are an administrator, network with your fellow administrators to organize one at one or more schools in your district on a scheduled professional learning in-service day.

Embrace the Three Cs: Communication, Collaboration, and Community

3

*Every successful individual knows that his or her achievement
depends on a community of persons working together.*

Paul Ryan

The 21st-century educator leads and models teaching and learning through connected, reflective, transparent, and collaborative methods. Such educators recognize that the educational landscape has changed with continuous advances in technology and see the benefits of transforming their role from a traditional isolated learner to a connected learner through the use of social media tools and a personal and professional learning network. They understand how connections developed through social media support them in cultivating a connected positive school culture and establishing a brand presence that extends far beyond the walls of their school community. They strive to build communities that currently do not exist, by communicating and collaborating with all members of the school community inside and outside their immediate circles in ways that foster cultures of excellence, in which everyone has the opportunity to become a part of something great.

It is important to note that educators who decide to go outside their own school communities to get connected and who have a desire to continue to grow professionally do so for different reasons. Some do so because they feel isolated from their peers or perhaps they are the only third grade teacher in their building. Others do so because they feel as though their peers either cannot or do not want to grow in the same manner they do and therefore are seeking other means to improve their craft. It is also interesting to note that many educators who are connected are extremely well respected outside their own organizations, yet their own school districts may not see or appreciate the value that a connected educator can bring to the local organization. This, in turn, perpetuates a feeling of isolation and the need for these educators to become even more connected because they feel their drive for a higher standard is either not appreciated or is not fulfilled. In the end, we must ask the question: Who is helping you get better, or—more importantly— who is inspiring you to want to be great? The challenge facing schools today is the ability to cultivate a culture wherein all members of the school community feel comfortable in disrupting routines long established by the status quo and embrace a connected world which is ready to support their desire to learn without limits.

▶ COMMUNICATING WITH PURPOSE

Today's educators have a vast library of free tools and resources available at their fingertips to tell not only their students' stories in the classroom, but also the stories of their schools. Tools such as Twitter, Facebook, Instagram, blogs, and podcasts are all available for free to support educators in getting connected in order to communicate their stories. Many connected schools today are utilizing Twitter in their classrooms/ schools to tweet out daily messages, showcasing the passionate work of their students and staff. By creating district, school, and classroom Twitter accounts, educators can share the passion they have for their school communities. In doing so, you may want to consider creating more than one school Twitter account, depending on the size of your school and programs in order to streamline your communication. Possibilities include an account for the principal, student club/activities, athletics, fine arts, and even a parent/booster account. Additionally, we highly recommend creating a school hashtag to create a connected community where students, staff,

> **66**By creating district, school, and classroom Twitter accounts, educators can share the passion they have for their school communities.**99**

parents, and the community can come together to connect and celebrate as one. Once you decide on a hashtag name, search this link: http://www.hashtags.org/ (#hashtags.org, 2014); click in the search box to see if your selected hashtag has already been taken. Oftentimes, if the preferred name is already in use, there is a simple way to make it your own by adding an additional character or two (if #LHS is already taken, for example, try #LHS2014). Once you have created a district, school, or group hashtag, start using these on all blog posts, tweets, and emails, and begin to encourage your students and families to do the same. Before you know it, a connected community emerges. Remember, the longer your hashtag, the fewer characters you have left from your original 140 characters, so it is important that your hashtag be as short and concise as possible.

One of the best examples of schools using hashtags effectively to create an engaged online learning community for their school originated with Jason Markey, Principal at East Leyden High School near Chicago, who worked with his school community to create the #leydenpride hashtag in order to bring a positive voice to his school community. Here is what Jason says about the power of the school's hashtag:

> Two years ago, at the same time we went 1:1 as a school by giving all students a laptop, I was having a conversation with two of our students about Twitter. At the time, students and staff were getting frustrated at how Twitter was becoming an avenue for sharing negative or even inappropriate comments. We decided instead of just burying our head in the sand, we should encourage and build a culture of participation in a conversation and celebration of our schools online by creating our own school hashtag, which became #leydenpride. Over the last two years this hashtag has become the place where our students, staff, alumni, and even parents go to be part of our school's conversation online, creating a voice for everyone in our community to share our story.
>
> (Markey, 2012)

To learn more about the Leyden journey, visit the link to Jason Markey's original blog post in 2012: Where is Your

School's Online Conversation? http://jmarkeyap.blogspot.com /2012/11/where-is-your-schools-online.html.

You can also visit the following link to a blog post by a #leydenpride student, Maja Bulka, who was a high school junior at the time she wrote this in February 2013: A Student's Perspective http://leydenlearn365.blogspot.com/2014/02/leydenpride-student-perspective.html (Bulka, 2013).

> **"**For connected educators, information flows quickly and efficiently, making communication convenient for all stakeholders.**"**

For connected educators, information flows quickly and efficiently, making communication convenient for all stakeholders. Whether through a 140-character tweet, a blog post, a Facebook update, or an Instagram photo and caption, school staff members can highlight students for their academic achievements, music performances, athletic accomplishments, service projects, and capture them at the very moment they are happening. This cultivates a sense of pride among the student body and school community as students are recognized for positive deeds that otherwise may have gone unnoticed. Through such communications, parents are also quickly notified or given reminders about important school functions such as open house, conferences, concerts, schedule changes, school cancellations, and security concerns. They are even given links to important resources which can benefit them or their children. In addition, when using Twitter to communicate news about school happenings, schools can link their school Twitter accounts and Facebook/Instagram pages so when a tweet is sent out it automatically embeds into the school's Facebook and/or Instagram pages. Social media tools such as Twitter, Facebook, and Instagram are readily available for free and are easily accessible for connected educators everywhere to use as professional tools to assist them in *communicating* what they want, when they want, and how they want.

▶ COLLABORATING WITH PASSION

In the opening pages of this book, we suggest that connected educators never lose sight of the fact that although connecting online in a variety of ways is an effective and efficient way of learning and growing professionally, nothing can compare with working and collaborating face to face with other educators. No amount of online connectivity can completely replace the power of meeting in person, but it can certainly play a vital role in building relationships with others around the world who share our sense of educational purpose and passion. Moreover, oftentimes what starts out as a virtual professional connection via Twitter, Facebook, Google Plus, or another online platform eventually becomes one in which PLN members meet face to face.

As an example, in February 2013, a group of connected educational leaders from all over the country who had originally "met" on Twitter decided to meet up in person at the National Association of Secondary School Principals' (NASSP) annual conference in Washington, DC. One day, as they were having lunch and sharing the great things that were happening in their respective schools, the conversation shifted to a discussion about what they could do as leaders to support their teachers in getting more connected so they, too, could benefit from a similar experience these leaders were having. As they chatted, they developed the idea of planning a teacher exchange program identical to what currently happens in schools with student exchange programs. The idea included teachers connecting through social media, traveling to the "exchange" district, hosting the teacher in their home in return, and, finally, spending the day at their "partner" school observing classrooms and exchanging ideas with one another. Although those involved in planning the idea were enthusiastic about it at the time, it was never acted on—until things changed during the summer of 2013.

During that summer, another group of connected educators arranged to meet in person in Kansas City. Jimmy was present for this dinner, as was Robert Sigrist, an assistant principal at Central High School in St. Joseph, Missouri. Here is what Robert shared about that encounter, one which ultimately resulted in one of the first teacher exchanges originally planned over a year before:

> Being connected via Twitter has given me the opportunity to interact with so many smart and talented educators. In the summer of 2013, a group of such educators met in Kansas City for an impromptu "BBQ Tweetup," giving me

the opportunity to meet many of these people face to face. During dinner, many of us were talking about the different issues facing us. I learned that Jimmy Casas's school was a 1:1 learning environment, with iPads as the device being used. This was something my school was also moving to and I shared with Jimmy that many of our teachers were worried because they were unsure how they were going to implement this technology in their classrooms. From our conversation at this dinner, Jimmy and I began to formulate a plan.

We were able to coordinate a "teacher exchange," whereby I traveled with several staff members to Bettendorf, Iowa, on a Sunday night. We stayed with members of Jimmy's staff in their own homes. We spent Monday at Bettendorf High School, where Jimmy serves as principal, seeing how they were able to incorporate this technology. Two weeks later, Jimmy and his teachers drove to St. Joseph, Missouri, on a Sunday night and we returned the favor, with several of our teachers hosting Bettendorf teachers in our homes and our school. Because of Twitter, not only were Jimmy and I able to connect with each other, but we were also able to expand that connection to teachers from our respective schools. Those staff members became key members of each other's PLN and serve as ongoing resources for each other. While we could have connected them through Twitter only, having the face-to-face connection was powerful. I know our staff gained valuable information from Jimmy's teachers, and I hope they were able to glean something from us as well. And it all started because of Twitter—and BBQ!

> 66As connected educators, we should strive to support our colleagues in our own schools, districts, and beyond in the learning process through collaborative means.99

As connected educators, we should strive to support our colleagues in our own schools, districts, and beyond in the learning process through collaborative means. Sometimes this entails challenging others to step out of their comfort zone in hopes that they will reflect on their own individual practices and experiences in order to learn and grow as educators. As we shared earlier and emphasize again in Chapter 4, being a connected educator is much more than just taking in: we must be willing to give back. One way to do this is by creating a personal blog. There are different platforms through which to create your own blog such as Blogger, WordPress, Tumblr, Posterous, and Habari, to name but a few. Before you decide which blogging platform to use, you want to keep these questions in mind to determine which might be best for you.

- Do I want to install, configure, and host my blog myself, or would I rather rely on a hosted service?
- Do I want to create my own blog theme, or am I satisfied with using or customizing an existing theme?
- Do I want to be able to install custom plug-ins or am I satisfied with the functionality that is built into the platform I choose?
- Will I be writing more long-form posts or posting cool things I find online? Or do I need to be able to do both?
- Do I want others to be able to comment on my post and interact with my content in a social way, or do I just want to be able to have a place to post my writing where people can read it and nobody can bother me?
- Am I willing to pay for this blogging platform?

(Dachis, 2012, para. 4)

If you are new to the world of blogging and thinking about starting a blog yourself, we recommend you begin by going through Google and using Blogger until you are confident that you are going to stick with it. Of course, you may choose to stick with this as your blogging platform permanently, but once you are comfortable with blogging and begin to get a better idea of your goals and your specific needs, you may want to explore the different features of competing platforms. Blogger will likely take care of most of your needs, and it is a free platform for blogging. Personal blogs can be formatted in many different ways, but you may want to consider including in your blog the following features:

- an "About Me" section
- a "Follow Me on Twitter" button
- a link to your Twitter feed
- a "Popular Posts" section

- a "Total Pageviews" button
- an option for readers to follow by email
- a link to your blog archive
- links to resources, articles, YouTube videos, and other information that may be of interest to your readers
- any awards you or your blog have received
- a "My Blog Lists" section

Connected educators all over the world are sharing their professional practices on their personal blogs and highlighting the tremendous work of their students and staff. They are handing out their "Top Lists" of best practices, tools, ideas, etc. so that others may learn by reflecting on their own practices. Others are showing their vulnerability by sharing publicly the mistakes they have made, fears they struggle to overcome, or the failures they have experienced. Finally, many take time to contribute personal stories or celebrate the successes of former students. As a way to get started, we encourage you to take time to visit the following blogs in order to connect with these incredible educators in various locations who support all educators on a daily basis by sharing their expertise and experiences through their blog posts. If you have yet to begin blogging yourself, we believe you will have a better idea of how to get started by reading these educational bloggers who have been at it for quite some time and who have inspired us with their writing and thinking:

> *Josh Stumpenhorst*—http://www.stumpteacher.blogspot.com/
> *Justin Tarte*—http://www.justintarte.com/
> *Tom Whitby*—http://tomwhitby.wordpress.com/
> *Joy Kelly*—http://joykelly05.blogspot.com/
> *David Culberhouse*—http://dculberh.wordpress.com/
> *Ben Gilpin*—http://colorfulprincipal.blogspot.com/
> *Richard Byrne*—http://www.freetech4teachers.com/
> *Bill Ferriter*—http://blog.williamferriter.com/
> *A.J. Juliani*—http://ajjuliani.com/

In June 2013, Jimmy was looking through his Twitter stream when he noticed a tweet from Jason Markey, Principal at East Leyden High School, asking followers to read a blog post which had been written by one of his students. When Jimmy clicked on the link, he noticed the blog site had been created to challenge members of the Leyden school community to write a blog post for each day of the year. As Jimmy began to read the posts, he was moved by the stories that were being told by members (mostly students) of the school community. He began to wonder how he could take this idea and adapt it to his school in order to bring his team of 145 staff members closer together and cultivate a community where people could get a better understanding of the work they each did every day on behalf of all kids. The following month Jimmy met with the team leader of the school counseling department to discuss strategies for the upcoming school year to more deeply engage students in learning and school. As he listened to the counselor share her philosophy and her story about how she worked to connect with students, it struck him that her words could be the beginning of a blog post.

In this way, the first blog post for what has become a venue for staff to share their expertise and stories, entitled "Breaking Down the Barriers," was authored by school counselor Amy Harksen. After deciding on a name for the blog, TSLG1440 (which stands for "Teaching, Sharing, Learning, and Growing Every Minute of Every Day, 24/7, and refers to the fact that there are 1,440 minutes in each day), the school staff began regularly contributing posts to the blog, showcasing their teaching, sharing, learning, and growing that took place every minute of every day. Jimmy began by approaching staff members individually to see if they would be willing to share, in writing, their individual stories and talents. Staff members could write on any topic they chose with the only stipulation being they had to make a connection back to their classroom. Initially, staff members were hesitant to post. Reasons included not feeling comfortable with their own writing, being afraid to "put themselves out there," not convinced they had anything important to share, and other reasons too many to mention. Interestingly, most teachers stated they lacked the confidence to write and felt the pressure of not presenting themselves in a positive light. However, once they actually finished writing and publishing a blog entry, every staff member who did so shared that they were glad they had written a post and had actually enjoyed their final draft once it was finished.

As the months passed, more and more readers began to follow the blog post. Staff were encouraged to participate through the principal's weekly Monday Memo, where he highlighted the weekly author. Team leaders were also encouraged to model the way by participating in the blog challenge. Blog posts were tweeted out weekly and comments received via Twitter were shared with the authors. A link was posted on the district website so members of the school community, including students, parents, community members, board members, and even prospective new families to the area could view the posts shared by members of the BHS staff. Staff members wrote with a sense of purpose and now anyone could get a glimpse into their thinking by reading about their personal stories and journeys. Creating a school blogging platform such as this one allows the school community to come together as collaborative colleagues. Teachers walking across campus will congratulate teachers in other departments on a job well done. Teachers will stop by the attendance office to tell the secretary how much they appreciated her work and her story. Paraeducators will receive words of encouragement when they share their stories and you can even invite retired teachers to jump into the mix to tell their stories. Even central office staff will likely make time to leave congratulatory comments on the blog.

The experience at Bettendorf High School with a "community" blog is but one of many examples and can easily be replicated at any school or in any school district. To take a look at how one school got started and how the movement grew, view the following link to the Bettendorf High School TSLG1440 blog, which can be found at http://tslg1440.blogspot.com/.

At the time of this writing, the blog included 38 postings written by 35 staff authors and has been accessed by over 20,000 readers from all over the world, including Australia, Japan, Canada, Algeria, Russia, Indonesia, Ukraine, India, China, France, Ireland, and Saudi Arabia. A community that had never before existed developed and grew through this collaborative blogging venture.

▶ COMMUNITY-BUILDING WITH PRIDE

One common theme that we have found to be true about connected educators is they have a tremendous amount of pride when it comes to telling the story of their schools. They find ways to leverage technology and incorporate it into the school community in a seamless fashion. No longer do parents have to ask or wonder what their children are doing at school on a daily basis. They already know because connected educators are using social media tools such as Twitter, Instagram, Storify, You-Tube, and other communication platforms to flatten the walls of the school so parents and the community can get a real and immediate glimpse of the countless and meaningful activities being experienced by students in schools every day. Whether you use pictures to show students working with their class-mates and teachers on a project, or share a video demonstrating the pride students have in expressing their passion for learn-ing, connected educators everywhere are making it a priority to highlight all that is awesome about their school communities.

Tony Sinanis (@TonySinanis), Principal at Cantiague Ele-mentary School in Long Island, New York, is one such principal who has created his own YouTube videos using the TouchCast app (see www.touchcast.com) to build his school's brand and bring his school community closer together. Here is what Tony says about the importance of building community by sharing your school's story:

> There are many ways to use videos to tell your story and build your brand! At Cantiague, we started doing Weekly Video Updates in which six or seven students from each class do research about what's happening on each grade level and then share those updates on camera. The chil-dren have two days to do their grade level research and then they join me for lunch and we make the video. The children are the best storytellers; who better to share what's happening in our schools than the people who are experi-encing it first hand—our amazing kids! That is the power of student voice (#stuvoice). These video updates have taken the idea of a newsletter and thrown it forward into the 21st century, helping to flatten the walls of our school and give the community direct access into the learning and teaching occurring at Cantiague. These updates have also changed the conversations during various community events and activities because now families are talking about what their

children are actually doing in school and they have a clear understanding of not only HOW we do things at Cantiague, but also WHY we do things at Cantiague. Our video updates have been a game changer!

For years, typical teachers and principals have lived professional lives marked by isolation, unconnected to any other educators outside their own school. They were limited in their communication, confined to a network of building colleagues, friends, family, community, and local media. This leaves schools at the mercy of others to tell their stories. This often leads to schools being viewed by many as challenging places where too much time and energy is spent on complaining about student behavior, lack of—or over-abundance of—parental involvement, shortage of resources, state and federal mandates, and so on. Sadly, what is lost in the translation is that others are not only listening, but they then, in turn, carry the same inaccurate and/or unfair messages and communicate these to others in the school community. Over time, these negative comments can become very damaging and begin to unfairly label a school as a poor-performing school with low morale, or worse yet, as cultivating a school culture that does not care about students. With the tools available to us now, it is easy to take the lead in ensuring that the story that gets told about our schools and our school districts is a story that is accurate and focused on the major, not the minor, happenings. How we share information can affect our school environments both positively and negatively. As the storytellers for our students and our schools, it is critical that we understand our role and intentionally plan how we communicate and share our story in a way that shows the pride we have in our school and our entire school community.

FOLLOW 5, FIND 5, TAKE 5

Follow 5: These five educators from our PLN stand as models in the area of the 3 Cs, which we have written about in this chapter. We have listed their names and Twitter "handles." We encourage you to follow these exemplary educators on Twitter and interact with them to enhance your life as a connected educator. Here are short pieces of advice from these experts in the field on the importance of Embracing the 3 Cs: Communication, Collaboration, and Community:

1. *Curt Rees (@CurtRees).* Elementary Principal, Wisconsin. Co-host of @TechlandiaCast. Curt participates regularly on #wischat, #cpchat, and #educoach. According to Rees,

Digital tools like social media services are excellent venues for building and enhancing positive culture within your school community. Countless successful activities are happening in schools every day, so make sure you take the time to share these events through platforms like Facebook, Instagram, and YouTube. Pictures and videos of smiling kids and teachers working together in an engaging project say a lot about your school. Make it a priority to share all that is good and right in your school.

2. *Chris Kesler (@iamkesler).* Eighth grade science teacher, Houston, Texas. Co-host of @eduallstarshq. Chris participates regularly on #tlap and #mschat. According to Kesler,

One of the most powerful things that I learned after getting connected with other educators outside of my school was the value of the 3 Cs. Once I embraced collaboration with my PLN, my world began to grow exponentially. I have been able to create projects that have made an impact on students and educators across the globe. Do not underestimate the power of connecting with others.

3. *Pernille Ripp (@pernilleripp).* Seventh grade English teacher, Madison, Wisconsin. Pernille regularly participates on #titletalk and #edchat. According to Ripp,

I didn't know I was unconnected, until I got connected. Then I realized the power of being a connected educator and what it meant for my students to be connected. Through our connections we have started global conversations, we have shared our messages, we have shared our hopes and dreams for the future. I created the "Global Read Aloud" so that others could find a way to become connected, and find their voice within the world. We are stronger, not just as educators, but as human beings when we reach beyond our classroom walls and invite the world in.

4. *Arin Kress (@ArinKress).* Fifth grade teacher in Grove City, Ohio. Arin regularly participates in #5thchat. According to Kress,

Communicating, collaborating, and building community effectively with students and teachers within your school and beyond is an important skill for every teacher to have. I have used Skype in the classroom to connect my students with others from around the world, most notably a fifth grade class in Perth, Australia. We communicate daily via email, weekly via shared video, and quarterly via Skype calls and shared packages. We collaborate on math and science projects and have successfully built a global classroom community. If you are just beginning your journey as a connected educator, it is important to remember to start small but always be open to working with others online. You will likely learn from one another and their insights will hopefully benefit your students.

5. *Tom Whitford (@twhitford)*. Elementary Principal in Tomah, Wisconsin. Tom regularly follows #atplc, #wischat, #IAedchat, #satchat, and #sblchat. According to Whitford,

We are living a world that continues to flatten, becoming more transparent and connected. We need to ensure that we are sharing the great things happening in our schools with our stakeholders so our mission and vision become evident. We need to make sure that the great minds in our schools are connecting with other great educational minds across our nation and even our world. As the saying goes, "The smartest person in the room, is the room." I have learned more from collaborating with great educators across the world than I ever have from a textbook or a lecture.

Find 5: We have found these five online resources/tools to be particularly useful in embracing the 3 Cs of Communication, Collaboration, and Community. The following links are resources that we have learned about via our PLN and that we have used ourselves to improve some aspect of our job performance or extend our thinking in this area:

1. 5 Effective Ways to Build Your School Tribe by @HollyClarkEdu http://www.edudemic.com/school-tribe/.
2. Check out these school/district hashtags on Twitter to understand the power of a community coming together to share their story. Simply type these hashtags into the search feature of Twitter or Tweetdeck and see what is being communicated via these school/district hashtags: #engage109, #bettpride, #leydenpride, and #gocrickets.
3. Leyden Learn 365 is a collection of daily posts about what is occurring at one school; for every day of the calendar year, you can click on the date to read about what students are learning—from students themselves! http://leydenlearn365.blogspot.com/.
4. How to Make a Blog on Blogger (tutorial): https://www.youtube.com/watch?v=Qa6MQxJOqv4.
5. Cantiague Elementary School YouTube videos: https://www.youtube.com/user/Teechman1.

Take 5: We conclude each chapter by recommending five action steps you can take to get started or continue as a connected educator. Here are five initial steps we suggest you take to get started with Embracing the 3 Cs: Communication, Collaboration, and Community:

1. Create a school Facebook page. Begin by posting three pictures a day that showcase all that is awesome about your school.
2. Open up a school Twitter account. Link your Twitter page to your Facebook page so that your tweets automatically embed on your

Facebook page. Set a goal to share at least five tweets about what is happening in your school or district each day.

3. Create a school hashtag. With the help of students, staff, and parents, encourage all members of your school community to include the hashtag in all tweets highlighting students or the school.

4. Create your own blog. Using Blogger, create a blog site, write your first blog post, and then share it with your school community or with the entire world via Twitter or Facebook.

5. Create a video highlighting your students and school and then upload the video to YouTube. Send the link to your P^{2}LN on Twitter.

Give and Take … and Give Some More

Takers eat well; givers sleep well.

Unknown

Connected educators give of themselves freely and often. This giving is typically in addition to the giving they do throughout the day during the normal course of their "regular" job, in which they are giving to the students and parents they serve as well as to the colleagues with whom they work. After a day spent giving in their daily workplace, they often go home and give some more professionally, by answering questions that have been asked of them by learning network colleagues near and far, by participating in online learning chats, by scheduling a video call with a colleague around the world, and by meeting up with learning network colleagues on a weekend to share ideas. The giving nature of a connected educator can be exhausting and grueling, but as the quote above suggests, such givers sleep very well at night, both literally and figuratively. Working this hard can be very tiring and requires that we remember the importance of balance in life, including enough hours of sleep each night. In a more figurative sense, giving educators sleep well at night because they know they are contributing not only to the organization they serve, but also to the education community as a whole.

Although connected educators are well known for their selfless acts of giving to individuals and to the profession in general, make no mistake about it: these educators are also interested in "taking." Although the quote above is intended to make fun of those who "take" in a selfish sense, and extolling the virtues of those who give freely, "eating" is every bit as important as "sleeping," and connected educators enjoy learning ("taking") from others just as much as they enjoy teaching ("giving"). Connected educators engage in a never-ending cycle of giving to others (whether by sharing a resource or offering to listen to a problem a colleague is having), taking back from others (whether by trying out an idea first learned of from a PLN member, or tweeting out a plea for help on a problem they are having), and then starting the process all over again by giving some more. Connected educators possess an almost fanatical "pay it forward" mindset, whereby they become energized not only by *giving*, but also by *receiving* help. Once they do receive help, they tend to become even more passionate about giving back in return and helping some educator, somewhere, become better in the process. It is probably fair to surmise that, in general, those who enter the education profession are likely to possess a giving nature and entered the profession in part to give back; this is what we love so much about the profession ourselves. Connected educators seem to possess this trait to an even more pronounced extent: the more they receive through their professional connections, the more they want to give—and the more they want to connect their colleagues to a similar network of people who are willing to support them regardless of their role in education, their location, or their current comfort level with reaching out to those beyond their immediate grasp to grow and learn.

▶ GIVERS PROMOTE PEOPLE AND IDEAS

One way that connected educators give is by promoting people they know in their learning network and the powerful ideas they come across via this network. These acts of promotion can be both small and large. The act of promoting other educators can vary depending on whether they are promoting an educator who is just starting out on their journey to become connected or is firmly established and recognized as a connected educator. Some of the most giving educators we know who are highly visible around the world as connected educators promote others simply by "following" them on Twitter or joining their Google Plus community. For every educator who embarks upon the journey to connect with other professionals and eventually finds the value in doing so, sticking with it and becoming passionately "connected," there are probably hundreds more who start out enthusiastically committed to doing the same, but who lose interest for one reason or another along the way. One simple step we can take to increase the chances that educators dipping their toes into the realm of connectedness take a deep dive is by following them on Twitter or other social networks when we know they are just starting out.

As we mentioned in Chapter 1, a common method that connected educators employ to get started is by building a learning network through Twitter. Unfortunately, for many who get started in this way, it takes time and effort to build such a network and begin reaping the benefits of doing so. Although the purpose of joining in the educational community on Twitter is certainly not to attract followers, it is equally true that if a teacher or principal has very few followers they soon lose interest in trying to connect. We have found that the "tipping point" in terms of followers for many educators who not only start, but also stick, with Twitter as a personalized learning tool is somewhere in the neighborhood of one hundred. Once you reach that number, the chances are fairly strong that you will see the benefits that can be realized by connecting in this way. Sadly, many educators give up before they get to that number of followers, disheartened by their lack of interactions with others on Twitter. Connected educators know that starting out to build a learning network can be difficult and can even be a waste of time unless you are following people who follow you back. As a result, connected educators tend to follow many of the educators who follow them, especially when they hear of someone who is just starting out and sincerely hoping to connect with others in an effort to learn.

Connected educators also promote people—and their ideas—by sharing what they learn from them with their own network. When they see that someone with whom they are connected has shared an idea that may help other

> **"**Connected educators also promote people—and their ideas—by sharing what they learn from them with their own network.**"**

educators in some way, they do whatever they can to spread the news about this idea. Often, it can be as simple as retweeting a link they saw to members of their learning network. It can be mind-boggling to learn how far, wide, and fast a tweet can travel. There are even Twitter analytic services (one example is TweetReach) to track the extent to which a tweet has "traveled." Using such a tool to test this out, we just learned that a tweet posted by a highly connected educator at the time of this writing reached 117,989 Twitter accounts within one week. This is powerful: if we learn an idea from someone in our network that we believe will better engage our kids in learning, for example, and then retweet that out to the world, it is possible that tens of thousands of other educators will eventually see this as well and be able to take advantage of the idea in their own school or classroom. Connected educators recognize the importance of promoting people and ideas as a way of giving back to the profession.

▶ GIVERS RESPOND

Connected educators have no more time in their day than any other living person; we each have available to us 60 seconds every minute, 60 minutes every hour, and 24 hours every day to get it all done. Therefore, these educators do not *find* time to give back (as there is no additional time to "find" in the 24 hours we are allotted each day); they *make* time to give back. One small, but important, way that connected educators "make time to make a difference" in the lives of other educators is simply by responding whenever someone reaches out with a question or with a plea for help.

Obviously, there are limits for all of us on how much time we have available to us, and on the many and varied competing demands upon this time. As a result, sometimes our response is simply a quick note to let someone know we cannot help at the moment or that we have no immediate ideas about a particular topic. Still, the power of taking the time to respond at all is real and it makes a difference to the person who has reached out. Often, of course, connected educators respond by offering support of some kind: they answer a direct question, send a link to a resource they think may help with the query, they direct them to someone else in their PLN who they know is an expert in that particular area, or they even pick up the phone to call the person to have a personal conversation about the issue. The bottom line, though, is that connected educators tend to respond when they are contacted about anything relating to their profession. Whether they ultimately end up helping or not with the initial request, they make time to answer directly and swiftly.

Because connected educators often have a significant number of followers and can be perceived as experts—at least in some aspects of education—other educators often turn to them for support or advice. They reach out in a variety of ways, either by emailing, calling, direct messaging on Twitter, or by commenting on a published blog post. In each instance, connected educators respond. They not only have a keen understanding of the needs of others, but they also empathize with them, as they have likely been in the same position before—and may find themselves in the same position again in the future. This give-and-take nature of connecting with members of our learning networks is a primary component to their power and success. Responding to others directly and swiftly is particularly important when it comes to supporting those who are new to the field of education—or who may be veteran educators but are new to the world of connected education. Although an obvious goal of connecting with others at all is to become better at what we do ourselves, another goal is to assist others in becoming better in turn. If we respond when someone reaches out, we give heart to the one who made the effort to reach out, and increase the chances that this person will continue to seek out new opportunities to learn, grow, and connect. Connected educators make our world a slightly better place by responding consistently whenever they are called upon.

▶ GIVERS CONNECT PEOPLE TO OTHER PEOPLE

An important way that connected educators give and take is by connecting members of their own network to each other and expanding their own knowledge and support base in the process. There are many times when connected educators are asked a question about an issue they may not be best equipped to answer. In such instances, connected educators stand ready to find someone else in their learning network who might better answer the question or provide support.

There are many ways that connected educators make time and find the means to connect colleagues they know in their own learning network to each other so that all may benefit. Of course, at times, this is simply a matter of phoning or emailing the person and asking for help and suggesting they contact an educator in their network who they suspect will have the expertise to assist. Other times, educators seeking to give help reach out first to the person they think can help and ask if they will reach out directly to the person needing it. Whatever the method, connected educators know that two heads are usually better than one and 2,000 heads are usually better than 200. As we have stated before, no single educator can ever know all there is to know about a topic. No matter how well versed we are on any topic, together we can always know even more. The good news is that there are literally thousands of educators ready and willing to lend their expertise if asked, typically swiftly and absolutely free of charge.

> **“**No matter how well versed we are on any topic, together we can always know even more. The good news is that there are literally thousands of educators ready and willing to lend their expertise if asked, typically swiftly and absolutely free of charge.**”**

As we have also stated, there are many ways that connected educators connect their learning network colleagues to each other. Currently, many do so through their Twitter PLN. As an example of the potential power of connecting educators around the world with each other, consider three members of our own learning network: Eric Sheninger (@E_Sheninger) is connected to over 64,000 Twitter followers at the time of this writing. Tom Whitby (@tomwhitby), another widely known and respected educator, is currently connected to over 49,000. George Couros (@gcouros), a highly regarded educational leader from Canada, is followed by over 55,000 members within his learning network. Although there are clearly some overlapping members within these sets of network members, it is safe to say that, in total, these three educators alone can reach out at a moment's notice to nearly 100,000 educators from around the globe. A fifth grade teacher in Kansas may be looking for support in the area of differentiating instruction for students in her diverse classroom. She can and should explore all available resources within her own school, including drawing on the expertise of colleagues in her own building. At the same time, however, she can simply tweet out a request for assistance on Twitter, asking educators like Eric, Tom, and George to retweet the request. Within hours, if not minutes, it is possible that her request for assistance will be seen by thousands of thoughtful educators around the world, many of whom would be eager to lend their support.

A favorite way that many connected educators give is simply by connecting a fellow educator in need to another fellow educator they know who might be able to provide the support, ideas, or resources needed. Once educators catch the bug that eventually happens as a result of connecting with others, it becomes a never-ending cycle of passing it along to others as a simple and effective way to grow and learn.

▶ TAKING BY STEALING, NOT BORROWING!

After Jeff's third year of teaching, he moved from teaching first grade in one school to teaching fourth grade in the same school. Being new to the grade level, he asked the veteran member of the fourth grade team and team leader if he could see her highly detailed lesson plan book from the previous year so he could use it to start planning his own lessons for his new grade level. To his surprise, the teacher somewhat angrily refused, telling him he needed to plan his own lessons. Times have certainly changed; back then, it was not uncommon to hoard ideas and resources, even from colleagues with whom you worked and whose friendship you valued. We believe that in most schools today, colleagues would be much more open to sharing their plan books—or anything else they have at their disposal—to help a colleague in need. To be fair to Jeff's colleague, however, she may have actually helped him to some extent: had she simply given him her plan book, he may have merely borrowed everything in there and not really owned it for himself. Like most connected educators we know, we would certainly advocate for sharing everything we can with our colleagues who ask for help. At the same time, it is incumbent upon the person seeking support to take away something from the exchange beyond the mere act of borrowing it to make their life easier.

As we mentioned at the outset of this chapter, connected educators tend to be truly giving people who seem to thrive on giving back to the education community whenever and however they can. At the same time, connected educators certainly are not opposed to "taking" as well and are always on the prowl to "take" by learning new and better ways to do those things they are passionate about doing. We know a colleague who is fond of saying, "Good teachers borrow from each other—great teachers steal." Although she says this as a lighthearted way to indicate how important it is to freely take ideas from others in an effort to not only get better but also to work smarter, not harder, there is a subtle, but significant difference connoted between the seemingly competing ideas of "borrowing" and "stealing."

Let us be clear: no connected educator we know becomes connected (at least, not successfully) simply so that they can selfishly steal ideas they learn of elsewhere, never giving back in return, and perhaps even claiming these ideas as their own. In fact, nothing could be further from the truth in our experience. However, just as genuinely giving educators get excited about sharing their ideas—and become even more excited when they see these ideas take root in other schools and classrooms around the world—they may be equally excited to "steal" an idea they learn from a PLN colleague, incorporating it successfully into their own practice. When each of us first started teaching, it was not uncommon for us to "borrow" from colleagues at our school with whom we taught. However, this borrowing often started and ended with *things* as opposed to *ideas*. Perhaps we needed some extra purple construction paper one day. The next week, we needed a worksheet to go along with the first few chapters of a novel we were teaching. Later, we needed some extra books for our classroom library as we began our unit on the planets. In these times, opportunities to connect with other educators were extremely limited. First, it started and stopped within the walls of our own school building. Second, the borrowing tended to be of material things; we rarely had collaborative conversations with our colleagues about ideas they had or ideas we had for better engaging our kids in a topic, lesson, unit, project one or more of us were teaching at the same time. Finally, whenever we did "borrow" something it was truly that—a transaction. We used something they had and would happily let them use something we had in return. The original item tended to stay with the original owner, even if the borrower used it, too. Our colleague who somewhat facetiously advocates for "stealing" over "borrowing" is suggesting that the first thing we need to focus on is exchanging ideas, not just things. More importantly, she is suggesting that we cannot truly get better just by "borrowing"—even if it is a really good idea one of our colleagues has started. Instead, we need to "steal" that idea and make it our own. We have been given the gift from a colleague—in today's world, that colleague may be either across the hall or across the world—who is willing to share with us. We honor this person not by taking what she has to share and using it exactly as designed, but by taking it, using it, strengthening it, and sharing it anew with others. We do not simply borrow; we own it for ourselves and add to it before giving it back again.

Connected educators thrive on giving—and actively seek out opportunities to do so. In addition, they are happy to take (even steal!) ideas wherever and whenever they can if it will help them do their current job better or help them add to their bag of tricks they can share with other educators at a later date when needed. When they do take ideas from others, it often becomes more than a simple give–take transaction. Instead, these events tend to be ongoing back-and-forth collaborative exchanges in which the original idea becomes improved over time through the giving and taking of not only the original giver and taker, but also an entire network of learners who in turn become exposed to the idea.

> **66** Connected educators are happy to take (even steal!) ideas wherever and whenever they can if it will help them do their current job better or help them add to their bag of tricks they can share with other educators at a later date when needed. **99**

▶ TAKING BY LOOKING OUT, NOT JUST IN

Connected educators are loyal to the organization they serve and desperately want the organization to become as successful as it can possibly become. They always start with their own classroom, school, or district in mind, asking, "How can I help to make this (classroom, school, district) even better than it already is?" They often begin by looking within their own organization, knowing that the best ideas frequently come from within and knowing that ongoing systemic school improvement must, ultimately, come from within, as Barth (2006) suggested.

At the same time, connected educators realize that it is also important to look outside the walls of their own classrooms, schools, and districts in order to capitalize on the good ideas of others and to learn what is working in other schools around the world. In today's era of connectivity, information is at our fingertips and immediately accessible, including finding out where things are already happening in education that we may be just beginning to think about implementing in our own schools. There are times when we advocate first starting within and then looking outside. Other times, we suggest starting by looking outward, then working from within. If we are working to get better at something we are already doing, we may start by working within—but also looking beyond. As an example, if we are examining our annual data, we may start by simply working within our professional learning communities already established in our schools, analyzing the data in every way possible, identifying areas of celebration as well as areas of future focus, and creating an action plan complete with SMART (Specific, Measurable, Attainable, Results-oriented, Time-bound) goals for improving future performance. Despite many changes in education, some things tend to remain the same and likely always will. Looking at our results and trying to achieve better results each year has become a staple of schools since the advent of No Child Left Behind (NCLB). Although NCLB is almost a thing of the past in many states, accountability for results remains—perhaps to an even more stringent extent than ever before. Owning student academic achievement results should start from within—all the while looking outside to see where others are achieving success and learning from them whenever possible.

On the other hand, when initiating something entirely new in a school or district, it sometimes makes sense to look outside the organization first and then build from within. Connected educators are more than willing to look outside their own classrooms, schools, and districts to do this. In today's ever-changing classroom environments, the number of examples of completely new ideas being considered for implementation is vast. For example, many schools arc making the commitment to a 1:1 learning environment for all students, providing a device of some sort for each student in the district in an effort to enhance teaching and learning. Other districts are taking a slightly different approach and instituting Bring Your Own Device (BYOD) policies, allowing individual students to bring their own devices to school with them to support their learning. Many teachers are trying new instructional ideas like the Flipped Classroom, Genius Hour, or Mystery Skyping sessions, to name a few. When taking on something entirely new for the very first time, connected educators know they stand a better chance of long-term success if they first look outside the organization to see where and how it is already working effectively elsewhere. Whether we are looking to implement 1:1 learning environments district-wide or incorporate Genius Hour into one fifth grade classroom, the place to start is the place where success has already been achieved. Connected educators around the globe are working in both locations; some are in a district hoping to start such an initiative, and others are in districts where the initiative has already taken root. The ones looking to start are never afraid to seek help from outside. Those outside who are having success are never hesitant to share.

Connected educators know that they must always be looking to grow and improve. They also know that neither they, nor anyone else in their own school district—no matter how stellar they might be—holds the keys to all the answers they seek. As a result, they constantly look outside their own organization to find new ways to improve.

▶ GIVERS, TAKERS, MATCHERS

Connected educators are passionate about giving and taking . . . and giving some more. Like the quote at the outset of the chapter suggests, givers sleep well each night, knowing they are contributing to the growth of others. Although they may tend to fall more on the side of giving than taking, they also enjoy "eating well" by taking ideas they learn from others in their networks and enjoying the benefits of adding to their repertoire of teaching or leadership techniques.

Grant (2013) explores the topic of giving and taking in great detail, studying highly successful people and determining the extent to which they give and take. He maintains that in addition to hard work, talent, and luck, successful people also thrive on connecting with others. Grant found that few of us are purely givers or takers and that we move from one role to the other depending on situations we face. Moreover, he found that a third role exists, one he terms "matchers," meaning people who help others but expect reciprocity in return. Although Grant found that the lines between acting as a giver, a taker, or a matcher are not hard and fast—he suggests that we shift from one style to another as we move from one situation or relationship to another—we do tend to develop a primary style in the workplace, a style that captures how we approach others most of the time in our work relationships. In our own experiences interacting and working with connected educators around the world, we have recognized even the most giving of educators moving between the three styles, acting as matchers or takers depending upon a given situation. Still, if Grant's findings hold true for connected educators, we would be willing to assert that the primary social interaction style for the vast majority is that of being a giver.

Interestingly, Grant found that "givers tend to sink to the bottom of the workplace success ladder, which may make us second guess our willingness to serve with a "give first" mindset" (2013, p. 6). However, before becoming too alarmed, you should also know that givers also are at the top echelon of success. In Grant's studies, although people exhibiting all three styles can and do succeed, givers are both the worst and best performers, while takers and matchers tend to land in the middle. In contrast to the success of takers and matchers, however, when givers succeed, it tends to create a cascading or ripple effect. Their success spreads to others; they enhance the lives of others through their giving. Connected educators are like the givers Grant describes: they succeed themselves and create a ripple effect throughout the education community, empowering others to succeed as well (Grant, 2013).

According to Grant (2014), when he first wrote his book, he attributed the long-term success of givers to two primary forces: relationships and motivation. Givers forged strong relationships with others, building deeper and broader connections. Giving to others also added meaning and purpose to their lives, motivating them to continue giving, and succeeding more in the process. Beyond relationships, though, Grant found learning to be a third reason why helping others resulted in distinct benefits for givers. By helping others in a variety of ways, givers are often learning in the process. If someone asks them for assistance, they may not immediately know as much as they would like to, so they learn some more about the topic before responding, or giving. In this way, connected educators who give freely learn more in the process and become even better equipped to give more—and grow themselves in the process.

Education is a giving profession by its very nature. We enter the field to help others, in particular, our students. Connected educators take this giving to another level, working intentionally to give to others—not only to the students they serve, but also to the colleagues they meet—by promoting people and ideas, by responding when they are called, and by connecting some members of their learning network to others they know. Connected educators are also always on the lookout for any good ideas or resources they can steal. They actively reach out to those within their own learning network for support and are always increasing their network of professional colleagues so that they have access to even more people, ideas, and resources from which to take—and to whom to give.

FOLLOW 5, FIND 5, TAKE 5

Follow 5: These five educators from our PLN stand as models in the areas we have written about in this chapter: their willingness to share of themselves and their eagerness to learn from others. We have listed their names along with their Twitter "handles." We encourage you to follow these exemplary educators on Twitter and interact with them to enhance your life as a connected educator. Here are short insights from these experts in the field on the value of serving as a connected educator and giving, taking . . . and giving some more:

1. *Nancy Blair (@blairteach)*. Principal, Rising Starr Middle School, Fayette County, Georgia. According to Blair,

It is not an overstatement to say that developing a PLN has changed my life, both personally and professionally. Through my PLN, I can learn, grow, and share with educators around the world. I can literally see into classrooms as teachers share what they are doing via live streaming. I can ask and answer questions from strangers who share an interest or passion. Over time, I've met face to face many members of my PLN who have become dear friends. It is an amazingly giving and supportive network.

2. *Paul Solarz (@PaulSolarz)*. Fifth grade teacher, Arlington Heights, Illinois. In addition to serving as a classroom teacher, Paul is a teacher-leader who shares his innovative teaching ideas with thousands of other educators around the world. According to Solarz,

By becoming active on Twitter, I have managed to connect with thousands of educators who are trying to do many of the same great things in their classrooms as I'm trying to do in mine. Through tweets, direct messages, email, and Skype, I'm able to collaborate with them directly by asking each other questions, sharing resources, and even connecting our students! In addition, weekly Twitter chats allow me to share what I'm doing in my classroom with a wide, authentic audience and they provide me an opportunity to learn about the newest trends, tech tools, and best practices from some of the most amazing minds in education. Being connected provides me with the best free, on-demand, differentiated professional development that I could hope for!

3. *Marcie Faust (@mfaust)*. Director for Innovative Learning, Deerfield, Illinois. According to Faust,

I believe that knowledge for the connected educator is like a giant snowball, beginning with a kernel of thought that becomes larger and more powerful as it gathers up bits of learning and experience from its surrounding community of educators. Like snowballs, educators do not grow just by sitting stagnant; they grow steadily by collecting wisdom from those around them. If we want to grow ourselves, we have a responsibility to learn from others and instead of giving back, we give forward, which strengthens the educational community of today as well as that of tomorrow.

4. *Erin Klein (@KleinErin)*. Classroom teacher, Michigan. MACUL 2014 Teacher of the Year. According to Klein,

Being a connected educator has supported me as a new teacher. Not only was I able to gain rich resources and ideas being shared, but I quickly gained a supportive network that I could turn to for questions and guidance. When I was new to teaching and new to social media, I joined #ntchat (new teacher chat) hosted by @teachingwthsoul (Lisa Dabbs). Lisa, a former principal, helped new teachers across the world to collaborate with one another and have a safe place to share their ideas and ask their questions. My insecurities began to diminish and my confidence began to grow. Having this global, connected network at my fingertips now shapes who I am as a teacher and enriches the ideas I bring into the classroom for my students.

5. *Garnet Hillman (@garnet_hillman)*. Instructional coach, Deerfield Public Schools District 109, Deerfield, Illinois. Garnet is a nationally recognized expert on the topic of standards-based learning and grading and co-moderates a weekly Twitter chat on the topic, #sblchat, which takes place on Wednesdays at 8:00–9:00 CST. According to Hillman,

As a connected educator I have learned that what you reap from relationships is interrelated with what you give. The more I give and provide to these relationships, the more I procure from the experience. When I write and share resources, I receive a variety of feedback that either affirms my thoughts or challenges me to improve my practice. I have grown exponentially as an instructor because of the wealth of knowledge my peers are willing to contribute to the world-wide educational conversation. I am grateful to my professional learning network as it delivers support and guidance any time I need assistance to innovate in my classroom.

Find 5: We have found these five online resources/tools to be particularly useful in reflecting on the power of giving and taking through your learning network. These are links to resources that we have learned about via our PLN and that we have used ourselves to improve some aspect of our job performance or expand our thinking:

1. An Interview with Stephanie Sandifer on How to Give to Get and More: http://connectededucators.org/profiles/interview-with-educator-stephanie-sandifer/.
2. Read about how one school organized their own professional development event by asking others around the world to participate in a Google Hangout panel. Building Capacity for Connected Educators at http://connectedprincipals.com/archives/7765.
3. Video: The Secrets of Success: An Interview with Adam Grant, author of Give and Take at http://live.huffingtonpost.com/r/segment/adam-grant-give-and-take/515a161e02a76031a90004b2.
4. Radical Openness: Growing TED by Giving It Away at https://www.youtube.com/watch?v=h3vZw08oP50.
5. Assess your social interaction style by taking a brief survey. Ask others to complete the survey based on their impressions of your style as well: Adam Grant's Give and Take website at http://www.giveandtake.com/.

Take 5: We conclude each chapter by recommending five action steps you can take to get started or continue on your path as a connected educator. Here are five steps we suggest you take to give to your PLN—and receive in return:

1. Consider an issue you are currently facing in your role as an educator for which you need some ideas. Ask three colleagues working in your school or district if they have any ideas which might help you. At the same time, send out a call for help via Twitter asking your online PLN to help and to retweet the request to others within their own learning networks.

2. Send out three tweets each day for one week, sharing three resources on the same topic each day. For example, on Monday, send out three different links to resources that can help teachers with math instruction. On another day, tweet out three resources that will help school principals hone their leadership skills.

3. Invite a fellow educator to observe you in action. If you are a teacher, ask a colleague to observe a lesson and provide feedback. If you are a principal, invite a principal from another district to observe one of your faculty meetings, and ask for feedback. Although you will receive great feedback from this, you will also likely be giving new ideas to the person(s) observing you.

4. Make time to visit another school or classroom you have learned of that is succeeding in an area in which you would like to grow. If you are a school or district leader, invite a team to accompany you on this visit. If you are a teacher, ask your principal if you can take a day to visit a classroom in a nearby school where there is a teacher doing something in their classroom you would like to learn about and share with others at your school.

5. Identify five things happening in your classroom, school, or district that you think are working well, helping students or staff to improve their performance. Find several different ways to share these five practices: blog about them, tweet them out, or highlight them at a grade level, faculty, or district meeting.

Strive to Be Tomorrow ... Today

*Success is a peace of mind which is a direct result of
self-satisfaction in knowing you made the effort to become
the best of which you are capable.*

John Wooden

In his book, *Teach Like a Pirate,* Burgess shares a famous quote by Jimmy Johnson, former coach of the Dallas Cowboys, that reads, "Do you want to be safe and good, or do you want to take a chance and be great?" (2012, p. 12). Maybe the better questions are: Who are you *allowing* to help you get better? What are you doing to help yourself get better? Are you surrounding yourself with greatness? Do you worry what others will think about you if you admit you want to learn more or be better tomorrow than you are today? In our lives as professional educators, we strive to inspire our students to believe they can achieve whatever success they set their minds to. But are we taking the time and doing the things we need to do for ourselves in order to be great? Some educators may have even settled for "average," as if they have accepted the idea that they do not deserve to be great. Well, we are here to tell you that you do deserve it and if you are going to be great and inspire your students and others to be great, then you must be willing to model what it looks like to push beyond the status quo and strive for excellence.

In our experiences, connected educators have this drive, this desire to want to be better, and a belief that they can change the world. They seek to connect and surround themselves with other educators who will challenge their thinking and cause them to stop and reflect on their own personal and professional practices and inspire them to strive for greatness! Connected educators embrace their vulnerability and extend their learning outside their comfort zone in order to make a broader and greater impact on their school communities and across global communities everywhere. They do not settle for where they are today as a limit to what they—or their schools—can become in the future. They make the most of each and every minute in the present, yet they are always keeping an eye out toward the horizon and an ear to the ground, anticipating what might be next for the field of education. As connected educators, they are leaders—whether they are leading from a classroom or an administrative office—and part of serving as a leader includes being at the forefront of change, always hoping that we can become even better tomorrow, regardless of how great we may already be today. Connected educators strive to be tomorrow . . . today!

> **❝**Connected educators embrace their vulnerability and extend their learning outside their comfort zone in order to make a broader and greater impact on their school communities and across global communities everywhere.**❞**

▶ SEEK THE POWER OF A POSITIVE VOICE

The truth is we are all powerful people who are blessed with powerful voices. Many connected educators have found that their voice can be a game changer for those with whom they connect, bringing about opportunities and inspiring students and teachers alike to believe they can change the world. They are not afraid to take risks and put themselves "out there," especially if it leads to deeper and richer opportunities for more students, staff, and the school community as a whole. There are connected educators across the country who believe that if they step up and take action they can transform the educational landscape for a community of educators everywhere. These people are often referred to as change agents. People like Jaime Casap (@jcasap), Google Global Educational Evangelist; Kristen Swanson (@kristenswanson), founder of the Edcamp movement; Tom Whitby (@tomwhitby), founder of #edchat; Scott McCleod (@mcleod), founding director of

CASTLE and Director of Innovation for Prairie Lakes AEA; and Jerry Blumengarten (@cybraryman1), creator of one of the most comprehensive educational websites available to educators, are examples of such change agents who have left their imprint on educators everywhere through both their actions and their voices. They are risk-takers, people like you and people like us, separated only by their courage to sit on the front porch rather than leave out the back door. Each of these leaders has a consistent and clear purpose, a vision of the footprint they want to leave on the world in which they live. They are passionate individuals who are determined to use their voice and their connectivity to influence change on a greater scale.

One way connected educators acquire a powerful and positive voice themselves is by seeking out as many positive and powerful voices they can from all walks of life. Such educators stay abreast of trends not only in education, but in all facets of our society by tuning in to what leading experts in a variety of professions are thinking, saying, and doing. An effective and efficient vehicle for keeping our fingers on the pulse of such new ideas is simply by watching TED (Technology, Entertainment, and Design) Talk videos. TED is a non-profit organization devoted to what they call "Ideas Worth Spreading" (TED.com, n.d.). TED started as a four-day conference in California almost 30 years ago and has grown to support world-changing ideas with multiple initiatives. The annual TED conferences invite the world's leading thinkers and doers to speak on a diverse mix of topics. Many of these talks are then made available, free, on their website. This is but one example of how using the power of a positive voice can impact educators all across the world. Many of these videos have become staples in staff meetings across the country because of their profound and inspirational messages on a variety of topics. One way educators can connect themselves to ideas and people they would otherwise be unable to and then, in turn, connect what they have learned to others in their PLN is by consistently monitoring the videos shared on this website and sharing ones they find meaningful with their learning network. There are hundreds

> **"**One way connected educators acquire a powerful and positive voice themselves is by seeking out as many positive and powerful voices they can from all walks of life.**"**

of TED Talks that are appropriate for educators for a variety of reasons. Among these, we recommend watching the following TED Talks, as a starting point, and sharing them with colleagues at your school and within your PLN:

1. Sir Ken Robinson: Do Schools Kill Creativity? at https://www.youtube.com/watch?v=iG9CE55wbtY.
2. Rita F. Pierson: Every Kid Needs a Champion at https://www.youtube.com/watch?v=SFnMTHhKdkw.
3. Angela Lee Duckworth: The Key to Success? Grit at https://www.youtube.com/watch?v=H14bBuluwB8.
4. Brene Brown: The Power of Vulnerability at https://www.youtube.com/watch?v=iCvmsMzlF7o.

Another series of videos that have become popular with educators as a way to lead not only for today but also for tomorrow are the heart-warming videos presented by "Kid President," because of his stated mission to "make grown-ups less boring." One of his most popular videos, entitled "A Pep Talk From Kid President to You" can be found at https://www.youtube.com/watch?v=l-gQLqv9f4o. This is another inspiring video to share with colleagues to discuss future trends we must consider in our profession.

What is intriguing about connected educators who are considered by their learning network colleagues as having the most profound impact on education today is that most have the ability to think long term as opposed to short term when it comes to defining what success looks like, and then working intentionally to achieve it. They throw out self-doubt whenever it begins to creep in, and stay the course, determined to make a difference in their lives as well as the lives of those they serve. They not only *want* to facilitate change for the better, they *believe* they will make a change for the better. They have managed to convince themselves that they are not necessarily *destined* for greatness, but *determined* to be great, regardless of the obstacles placed before them. They expect that the results they aim to attain will happen, in part, simply *because* they expect them to happen. These so called "powerful" connected educators are not afraid to share their voices in a public domain whether through Facebook, Twitter, books, blogs, websites, or face to face. They speak the truth when given a chance to stand before an audience at a conference or share their insight on a panel. Where others around them may fall prey to focusing on the "noise," they find the positive voice left in the comment section, tweet, or blog post, and view it as a learning opportunity from an extended network of experts. They do not allow failure or gossip to define them and they approach every challenge as an opportunity to rise above the noise in order to make a significant impact on what they can control.

▶ BRING YOUR PERSONAL BEST EVERY DAY

In order to anticipate and plan for tomorrow, one must live fully in today. A huge part of striving for a successful *tomorrow* is by living out a great *today*. No matter how excited some connected educators might get about what is coming down the pike in the future that may hold the power to transform what they are currently doing for the better, they know that they must make the most of every day and choose to bring their best game to what they do "ten days out of ten" (Whitaker, 2004, p. 43). Every day can be a great day if you choose to make it a great day. You are not going to be able to control everything that happens to you on a daily basis, but you can control how you let it affect you and your demeanor. It is your decision, and yours alone, whether to strive for greatness each and every day. Make a choice. We have all heard this line a thousand times: "ATTITUDE . . . is yours worth catching?" These five simple words serve as a reminder that your day will be what you make it to be. Educators around the world are connecting and interacting on Skype, Google Hangout, Twitter, Edchats, and a host of other outlets on a daily basis with other educators who are just as committed and passionate about making a difference and using their energy to fuel them and inspire them to strive to be the best they can be. When educators spend time connecting and cultivating both personal and professional relationships with other educators, it causes them to reflect on their own practices, thus leading them to question their own thoughts, behaviors, and expectations about how they regularly interact with others in their own organization on a daily basis. Ultimately, as a result of this ongoing cycle of reflection,

many choose to raise their own personal standards and surround themselves with excellence in order to become excellent
themselves.

In the field of education, we often hear the term "best practices." Typically, we invoke this term when we are citing research
studies which show that here are certain practices we can
employ or steps we can take to improve our instruction and, in
turn, improve student outcomes of some sort. Although clearly
important and critical to our core business of student learning,
we are even more passionate about another set of best practices: best practices for bringing your personal best each and
every day. Based on our experiences working with great educators around the globe who serve in a variety of roles, a few
such "best practices for bringing your best" include the following intentional behaviors that connected educators who make a
difference embrace:

- They bring their best to their organization every day,
  whatever their best may be that day. They are grateful
  for the opportunity to make a positive impact on a child
  every day.
- They are intentional with their time and make the effort to
  connect personally with students and staff on a daily basis
  and then follow up with a quick word or note. They realize
  that even the smallest gesture of kindness can make all the
  difference to the person to whom it was extended.
- They are empathetic. They take time to understand, share,
  and be sensitive to another person's feelings in order to
  foster a culture of trust. They recognize that every student and staff member will face some sort of personal and
  professional challenge at some point in time and they are
  sensitive to this fact.
- They value mistakes and failure as learning opportunities.
  When they themselves make a mistake, they own it, apol-
  ogize, and work to make sure it does not happen again.
  When they fail, they reflect on the experience as a way to
  see what they can learn for future attempts.
- They model forgiveness—they are sincere in accepting
  apologies and moving on. They believe that most people's
  intentions are good.

- They understand they will not always see immediate results when working with kids. They are patient and think long term. They do not take things personally. They have figured out that many kids are just testing a system which had failed them long before that particular teacher came into the picture.
- They have high standards for all kids every day. They do not make excuses for kids based on race, socioeconomic class, environment, or poor parenting. They truly believe in all kids all of the time and, more importantly, they love them as though they were their own.
- They acknowledge inappropriate behavior of kids. They understand that by not doing so, they are sending a message that the misbehaving student is not worth their time or that they have given up on them. They have come to learn that if they hesitate to correct poor behavior, they have become part of the problem.
- They bring positive energy every day. They know that complaining and talking negatively about kids, staff, or the work environment without offering a solution says more about them than it does about who or what they are complaining about.
- They take time to smile and laugh and encourage others to have fun.

Most people who choose to go into education as a career do so because they want to make a difference. They enter the teaching profession believing they can make a difference and with a sense of optimism that is refreshing. And then somewhere along the way, they may begin to question whether all the time, effort, and stress is really worth it. Occasionally, connected educators even begin to feel somewhat alienated from their colleagues in their own work environments. Ironic, is it not? What does it say about our profession when educators who strive to be the best at what they do in order to give back to others begin to suffer the backlash that comes from wanting to be successful? In many instances, educators who make the decision to connect and network beyond their school organizations to become the best they can possibly become are labeled as arrogant, self-serving, self-promoting, or too good for the rest of the team. Other team members may begin to make comments about their "Twitter friends" or use a negative tone when referring to anything that has to do with their PLN. Recently, a well-respected connected teacher who is viewed as excellent by other connected educators was presenting at a national conference. She had just finished "wowing" the crowd with a powerful message which demonstrated her expertise and knowledge, providing relevant examples for audience members to learn from and take back to their respective schools. What was interesting was that no one back in her home school had ever seen her present or asked her to share her expertise with educators in her own district, yet here she was on a national stage engaging, inspiring, and empowering a roomful of educators from across the nation who did not know her personally. Here stood this teacher with a tremendously high skill set, valued, respected, and admired by her PLN and non PLN educators, yet ignored and sometimes even knocked down by her own co-workers. Connected educators lean on their PLN during these difficult times to persevere and push through. Making the decision to reach beyond the walls of your own workplace or school community to learn and grow—somewhat ironically, we think—may create feelings of resentment within some of your colleagues. When dealing with any such negative pushback, consider these four points by Hall of Fame UCLA softball coach Sue Enquist. As Enquist said, "Personal excellence starts over each day" (as cited in Casas, 2013, para. 5). She reminds us that each day is truly a new day to be great and what you do with it is up to you:

1. *33% Rule:* Don't let the bottom third suck the life out of you. The bottom third includes those individuals who either can't or won't celebrate your successes with you. For whatever reason, those who live in the bottom third cannot be genuinely happy for others when they experience any amount of positive attention or are recognized for their accomplishments. They tear others down through their negativity and, in many instances, relish in others' personal failures. These people not only want to remain status quo, but they judge others who strive to move beyond and become better. Surround yourself with

a circle of excellence in order to protect your greatness! (Enquist, 2013, para. 3)

2. *Don't Allow Anyone To Take Away Your Excellence:* This is one of the most difficult challenges we face in our daily lives as connected educators. Our society is filled with mediocrity. You deserve so much more. It is easy to be duped by mediocre disguised as good. Just as success breeds success, it takes excellence to recognize excellence. We have too many individuals who are simply waiting for tomorrow when they can become excellent tomorrow by being excellent today. Truthfully, it takes courage and a strong will to be excellent, because there are always many mediocre people waiting to bring you down. Bring your excellence every day and don't let anyone kidnap your best and hold your greatness hostage! Remember, "Excellence doesn't negotiate!" (Enquist as cited in Casas, 2013, para. 4)

3. *Accept That You Will Fail, So Recover From It Quickly:* Our internal attitudes determine how quickly we can recover from failure. What is your inner voice saying to you? Is it saying that something isn't fair? Is it telling you that you can't do something? Is it telling you that you are overwhelmed? The fact is we fail every day, but our failure doesn't have to define us, especially if we aspire to be great. (Enquist as cited in Casas, 2013, para. 5)

4. *Personal Board of Directors:* Ask yourself today, who would be on your personal board of directors and who would you list as the Board Chairperson of your personal and/or professional life? Are these individuals helping you achieve greatness? Are they advancing your life goals? Who would you include? Are the people you would list representative of the legacy you want to leave behind? When dealing with difficult colleagues, it is not only important, but necessary, to make sure you surround yourself with others who want the best for themselves—and for you. (Enquist as cited in Casas, 2013, para 6)

Challenges like the ones described in this chapter are all too common in schools today. Perhaps just as challenging is how we can help school personnel remain positive on a daily basis

> **❝** It is neither our successes, nor our failures, that define who we are; rather, it is the choices we make and how we respond that define us. **❞**

so they can continue to always bring their best. We must start by recognizing that it is neither our successes, nor our failures, that define who we are; rather, it is the choices we make and how we respond that define us. How we respond begins and ends with us. So, how will you respond the next time someone asks you if you want to be the best at what you do? Whatever you decide, your response is the practical measure of your own level of excellence. Connected educators call on an inner strength and fortitude and enlist an army of supporters to ensure that they bring their personal best each day.

▶ STRIVE TO MAKE A GREATER IMPACT

In June 2013, Adam Bellow (@adambellow) was the keynote speaker at the International Society for Technology in Education (ISTE) Conference in San Antonio, Texas. During his speech, entitled "You're Invited to Change the World," Adam talked about his Change the World (2012) charity campaign: https://www.youtube.com/watch?v=3yh5gVCx0LA that allows viewers to click an image of a penny on the website; in return, Adam and his wife donate one penny for each click, with the rest of the donations coming through a method called crowdsourcing. The money collected through this effort is contributed to a worthy charity voted on by participants in an effort to, well, change the world. The point Adam shared was not about making money, of course, but about how small things add up, that small change matters, and that together we can change the world. Our experience with connected educators all over the world is that they fundamentally believe that together they can change the world—one tweet, one blog, one contribution at a time. Taking time to explore resources, craft ideas, share knowledge, and, most importantly, take action is what we have observed connected educators doing as part of their mission to create life-changing moments not just for themselves, but for the students, colleagues, and other educators whom they have never met face to face but with whom they share a bond that is as strong as a childhood friendship. They are not afraid to surround themselves with others who have the same aspirations and in some cases even greater aspirations in order to push themselves to a higher level. They listen to others who may have more experience, expertise, or even a higher skill set than they do about a particular topic and then allow their thinking and past practices to be impacted in positive ways. Over time they begin to allow their core fundamental belief system to be influenced in ways they could never have imagined in order to grow and develop not only as thinkers but also as *doers*.

Connected educators are greatly impacted in such ways because they are collaborating with more people than ever before via online spaces and collecting new ideas and activities from their P²LN to bring back into their classrooms and school organizations. They have figured out that they have an abundant amount of resources available to them at their disposal that they would never have had access to or found if left solely to their own devices. As Amber Teamann (@8amber8) has shared many times in her talks, "The smartest person in the room is the room" (A. Teamann, personal communication, September 1, 2014), meaning, in effect, that no single person in the room has all the answers; rather, it is the collective synergy and passion among all those assembled within the room (whether the room is a traditional one or, perhaps, a virtual one) that holds the keys to success. In fact, an ever-growing number of connected educators across the globe are sharing similar stories of how inspiring, invigorating, refreshing, and meaningful their work has become since they surrounded themselves with others who share their same passion to make an impact on a daily basis. They wake up each morning looking forward to going to work and ready to make a difference. They are more positive, engaged, informed, and present in conversations with colleagues and with others around them. They have become a go to source for their colleagues who are looking for new ideas and resources.

There is an endless number of ways that such educators are leading like this, striving to make a greater impact by taking what they receive from their learning network and translating this learning into actionable steps in their own schools or districts. After being motivated to make the greatest impact they can make—oftentimes from someone outside their own organization—they respond by doing just that: planning intentionally to make a positive impact in the lives of those with whom they work most closely. Here are a few of our favorite ideas for making this happen; although many of them require the participation of a school leader in a *formal* role of authority such as a building principal, the idea for initiating many of these events often comes from teachers who have learned about them via their PLN:

1. *Speed Meet and Greet:* Create a "speed-dating-like" activity with a variety of questions as an icebreaker to connect your staff and focus on cultivating a family culture that stresses the importance of relationships.

2. *Make it Personal:* Give teachers an allotted time during a professional learning day to make five personal calls to parents whom they typically would not contact and ask them to share with the parents something specific that is awesome about their child. Then have teachers record the responses from parents and share out to the entire staff all of the positive comments that were received as a result of this gesture.

3. *The Welcome Wagon:* Have a select group of staff meet with every new student to the school and ask them about how their experience has been as a new student being welcomed into a new school community. Then share those responses with staff at a faculty meeting.

4. *Making Invisible Students Visible:* During your back-to-school meetings, put a list of every student in your school on the wall and have the staff write a positive note to each student. As each comment is written, take down the student's name and at the end you will know which students are *invisible* as they walk the corridors of your school. Use this information as a way for your school team to cultivate a relationship with a student whom not many people know.

5. *This Week on Twitter:* Include a "This Week on Twitter" section in your weekly communication to staff, with thought-provoking tweets, blog posts, videos, graphics, and other resources.

6. *Thank a Parent—or a Staff Member:* Take a day or two to call the parents of your new teachers and let them know how wonderful it is having their son/daughter working in the building.

7. *Two a Day:* Write two personal notes every day to staff members in your building. By the end of the week you will have brought a smile to ten staff members and 40 smiles in one month.

8. *Invite Them Back:* Contact any students in your school who have dropped out and personally invite them back. Let them know how much you care and ask them what it will take for you to support them to earn their high school diploma.

9. *Accentuate the Positive:* At your next administrative meeting talk about a teacher who has made tremendous progress this year. Substitute the negative talk with positive success stories in order to model and cultivate the culture of excellence we all strive for in our buildings/organizations. Then follow up with a note to that teacher.

10. *Celebrate Good Times:* Begin each faculty meeting with positive stories about children shared by your teachers. Take time to celebrate even the smallest successes of each child.

11. *Front and Center:* Have the principal put her desk out in the main entrance of the school periodically so that every person who enters the school will get a personal greeting from the principal.

12. *Student Leadership Teams:* Create a student leadership team and host a monthly luncheon with them to discuss what you can do together to create a school culture of excellence.

13. *Exchange Dates:* Host a student and teacher exchange with other schools so you can model the importance of connecting and learning from others outside your school organization.

14. *Local Edcamp:* Partner with a neighboring school district and collaborate/participate in an Edcamp professional development day together.

15. *Televise the Tweets:* Place a television monitor in your school to capture and highlight tweets from students and staff.
16. *#oneperson:* Have all staff members write down someone who made a difference in their lives on an index card and have them include the address of that someone on the postcard. Collect the postcards and store these in a safe place until December. At that time, send a letter to your staff member's #oneperson identified on the index card.

Several times throughout this book we refer to the power of Twitter, which currently stands as the primary tool or vehicle for many, if not most, connected educators to become and remain connected to a boundless world of people, ideas, and resources. However, we also recognize that those individuals who "strive to be tomorrow. . . today" know that tomorrow may be a different story, whether we are talking about a month from now, a year from now, or five years down the road. Connected educators who strive to be tomorrow today have a mindset that there is always more to learn and they are able to anticipate the next thing coming at them. In doing so, they are cognizant of the fact that is never about the "thing," but rather the "thing" is simply a tool to help get them where they need and want to go next in order to make a greater impact. We would equate this to the 1:1 learning environments that many schools are moving towards. We must continue to communicate the message that it is not about the device, but rather the transformation of instruction and the authentic learning experiences and opportunities that arise as a result of having a device readily available as a resource tool. The same can be said about Twitter, Facebook, Voxer, or any other tool that supports and encourages digital connectivity. We know that tomorrow will be different than today; learning is never about one thing and the best experiences are still found in the personal connections we make with others who have similar aspirations to change the world for our children. Those who strive to be tomorrow today know that success and a positive mindset begins with not just a *can do* attitude, but a *will do* attitude. It takes courage and grit to harness the power of a positive voice, to bring your personal best every day, and to make an intentional, persistent effort to make a greater impact above and beyond what is merely required.

FOLLOW 5, FIND 5, TAKE 5

Follow 5: These five educators from our PLN stand as models in the areas we have written about in this chapter: never forgetting that everyone has the capacity to lead and that our kids deserve for us to bring our very best to work every day! We have listed their names along with their Twitter "handles." We encourage you to follow these exemplary educators on Twitter and interact with them to enhance your life as a connected educator. Here are short insights from these experts in the field on the value of serving as a connected educator who strives to be tomorrow . . . today!

1. *Matt Townsley (@mctownsley).* Director of Instruction and Technology, Solon, Iowa. Former moderator of #iowacore. Matt regularly follows #IAedchat, #sblchat, #iaedfuture, #commoncore, and #tlchat. According to Townsley,

I cannot imagine being in education without a connected group of colleagues to lean on for advice and inspiration. Prior to connecting with educators through Twitter and other social media tools, I counted down the days until the next education conference in which I might meet a new person to come alongside or mentor. Today, I look forward to those same conferences, but instead, for a different reason: to put a face to a name of those from whom I learn every day. I am indebted to my brother-in-law, also an educator, for showing me the value of Twitter as an educational tool and RSS feeds as an efficient way of curating news, blog posts, and other educational wisdom.

2. *George Couros (@gcouros).* George is the Division Principal of Innovative Learning for Parkland School Division in Edmonton, Alberta, Canada. According to Couros,

Social Media has become a great way to connect with the best educators that are actually in schools and doing the work. We are not waiting years for research, but sometimes only until the end of the day, or even learning while things are happening. It is a great way to learn from anyone and everyone to make our schools better today.

3. *Maggie Bolado (@mrsbolado).* Maggie is a sixth grade science teacher at Resaca Middle School in Los Fresnos, Texas. Maggie regularly follows #aledchat, #stemchat, #satchat, #satchatwc, #leadwithgiants, and #flipclass. According to Bolado:

Teacher connectivity is about relationships. I am the lead learner in my classroom and in fulfilling this duty, I bring forth the best thinkers around the world into a small room at Resaca Middle School to positively impact what my students experience there. Whether I am facilitating a vocabulary project or a collaborative multi-media project, the results are demonstrations of my students' critical thinking and communication capabilities. Connected learners take on a micro-blogging challenge whose mission is to maximize the learning experience beyond the class-room. Mission accomplished.

4. *Dave Burgess (@burgessdave)*. Dave is a professional develop-ment speaker and trainer, publisher, and author of *Teach Like a Pirate*. Dave is the founder and moderator of #TLAP and regularly follows #sat-chatwc, #scitlap, and #sstlap. According to Burgess,

Twitter is the best source for 365/24/7 access to completely personal-ized professional development with no geographic barriers, collaboration with the most innovative educators in the world, and . . . it's free! The key to unlocking the treasures of Twitter is the hashtag. Finding the right hashtags can change your professional life.

5. *Salome Thomas-El (@Principal_EL)*. Head of School, Thomas Edison Charter School, Wilmington, Delaware. Principal El has guest moderated on several chats including #IAedchat, #satchat, #usedchat, #thetitleonechat, and #christianeducators. He also started a running group on Twitter called #500in2014. According to Principal El,

As school leaders, it is critical that we model transformational change and develop powerful learning environments for our students and teach-ers. We must challenge educators to become leaders of change who embrace global connectivity for all students. Our role is to serve as cham-pions for our students, teachers, and families so they feel like they have a meaningful role in their school communities. We must take advantage of the social media tools available to us today to recognize and celebrate the amazing talents of our children. As servant leaders we must stop praying for a lighter load and start praying for a stronger back . . . there is more work to be done!

Find 5: We have found these five online resources to be particu-larly useful in reflecting on the power of finding a more positive voice from within members of your PLN. These are links to resources that we have learned about via our own PLN and that we have used ourselves to improve some aspect of our job performance or expand our thinking in this important area:

1. Sue Enquist: 33% Rule at https://www.youtube.com/watch?v=SXQ2MdlwHrl.
2. Byron Reese: Achieving Greatness is a Choice at https://www.youtube.com/watch?v=XfCaArxitpM.
3. Marc and Angel Hack Life: Practical Tips for Productive Living at http://www.marcandangel.com/.
4. Jamie Casap: Saving the Silver Bullet at https://www.youtube.com/watch?v=FbXgCLMl9R4.
5. Drew Dudley: Leading with Lollipops at https://www.youtube.com/watch?v=hVCBrkrFrBE.

Take 5: We conclude each chapter by recommending five action steps you can take to get started or continue on your path as a connected educator. Here are five steps we suggest you take to make a greater impact in your organization or your community by learning with your learning network colleagues:

1. Create a list of individuals that you would include on your Life Board of Directors. Who would you list as the CEO? Next, create a list of characteristics that you admire about them and strive to emulate them, while staying true to yourself.
2. Select two items from the list of 16 suggestions listed in this chapter on how to make a greater impact, and make a commitment to follow up and take action on these two items.
3. Submit a proposal to present at a regional or national conference. If selected, work with members of your school team or PLN to include them in the presentation.
4. Organize your own Edcamp. You can do this within your own building, district, with neighboring schools, or within your own state. Here is a link to the complete guide on organizing and running your own Edcamp at http://edcamp.wikispaces.com/file/view/HowToEdcamp.pdf.
5. Host your own Twitter chat. Team up with a member of your own PLN in order to grow your network and inspire others to embrace change. 5 Steps to Hosting Successful Twitter Chats: http://www.socialmediaexaminer.com/twitter-chat-guide/.

Know That It Is Still About the 3 Rs: Relationships, Relationships, Relationships

6

If moral purpose is job one, relationships are job two,
as you can't get anywhere without them.

Fullan, 2001, p. 51

In Whitaker and Zoul, we suggested that nothing in our profession is as important as relationships, by stating, "If the three most important words in real estate are 'location, location, location,' an equivalent in the realm of schools would be 'relationships, relationships, relationships.'" (2008, p. 78). The importance of intentionally building and maintaining positive relationships with our colleagues simply cannot be overstated. All successful educators know this and work to establish positive relationships not only with the students they teach, but also the parents of the students they teach, and the colleagues with whom they work. This focus is not a variable between *connected* and *unconnected* educators; both groups of educators are masters at focusing on and forging positive relationships. The difference, however, lies in the fact that connected educators have an additional network of people with whom they interact regularly and with whom they also establish positive, productive relationships: members of their learning network who work beyond the walls of their own school and/or district.

The research on the necessity and power of excelling in the area of relationships is vast. When writing about emotional intelligence, Goleman, Boyatzis, and McKee (2002) emphasized the importance of relationship management. Marzano, Waters, and McNulty (2005) identified relationships as one of the 21 responsibilities school leaders must fulfill to positively impact student academic achievement. In discussing the concept of the *soul at work*, Lewin and Regine stressed the importance of relationships as a way to feel more connected to a deeper purpose, resulting in a feeling that "they are part of a greater whole, a web of connection" (2000, p. 27). In the classroom, of course, relationships are of paramount importance. In a meta-analysis on student-centered teaching, Cornelius-White (2007) found that the essence of a student-centered teacher consists of the teacher exhibiting warmth, trust, empathy, and positive relationships. Barth (2006) wrote about the importance of establishing both *congenial* (polite, friendly, positive) relationships with our colleagues as well as *collegial* (collaborating and conversing about our practices as educators) relationships. Finally, leadership experts Kouzes and Posner (2003a) emphasized that caring about those with whom we work is essential to our effectiveness. They established a framework for cultivating and maintaining positive relationships that consists of seven keys: (1) setting clear standards, (2) expecting the best, (3) paying attention, (4) personalizing recognition, (5) telling the story, (6) celebrating together, and (7) setting the example. These seven characteristics of positive relationship building are central to the success of educators everywhere, from those serving in urban settings to those serving in remote, rural areas. Although successful educators are found everywhere excelling in these seven areas, we have found that they are especially pronounced in the lives of connected educators.

> 66 Relationships are of vital importance in the lives of all educators; we are in, perhaps, the most people-oriented business of all, and, ultimately, it is our people not our programs that will dictate our level of success. 99

Relationships are of vital importance in the lives of all educators; we are in, perhaps, the most people-oriented business of all, and, ultimately, it is our people not our programs that will dictate our level of success (Whitaker, 2004). Educators who make the biggest difference in the lives of the students with whom they interact are likely the ones who have established the most positive relationships—not only with the students themselves, but also with the other educators to whom they are connected within and beyond the walls of the school(s) they serve. Connected educators work intentionally to establish positive relationships with their immediate co-workers; they also seek out professional colleagues around the globe with whom they can exchange ideas, share stories, grow, and learn and are equally focused on the relational aspect within these interactions. They make time to regularly connect with members of their learning network via social media platforms, but they also find ways to meet in person to connect face to face whenever possible. Finally, connected educators look for ways to get the students in their schools and classrooms more connected to other students in other schools across the globe. They know that being connected is important for them personally and professionally and should be equally important for the students they serve. Although this chapter focuses on the connections we make as educators and the relationships we build through these connections, it is also important to note that many connected educators have extended this world of connectivity, connecting not only as educators, but also by connecting their students to students around the world through Twitter, Skype, blogging, Google Hangouts, and other means.

▶ IT STARTS WITH TRUST

Bryk and Schneider (2002) were able to establish a connection between the level of trust in a school and student learning. In short, their work indicates that although trust alone does not guarantee success, schools with little or no trust have almost no chance of improving. Bryk and Schneider (2002) found that schools with a high degree of relational trust are more likely to raise student academic achievement compared to schools with lower relational trust. They list four signs of such trust: (a) respect, (b) personal regard, (c) competence

> ❝ Schools with a high degree of relational trust are more likely to raise student academic achievement compared to schools with lower relational trust. ❞

in core responsibilities, and (d) personal integrity. In another study, Sebring and Bryk (2000) found that schools indentified as improving score high on levels of trust and cooperation among adults in the building, with students reporting that the adults care about them. On the other hand, in schools experiencing declining or flat scores, teachers are more likely to say that they do not trust one another. Clearly, trust is at the center of all relationships. We develop deeper and long-lasting bonds with those people who we trust. There have been several studies conducted examining what constitutes trust and how to determine its existence. Tschannen-Moran and Hoy (1998) identified five key components to measure trustworthiness:

1. Benevolence—those working together have each other's best interests at heart and will protect those interests.
2. Reliability—those working together can depend upon each other to come through.
3. Competence—those working together believe in one another's ability to perform the tasks required by their positions.
4. Honesty—those working together can be counted on to represent situations fairly and with integrity.
5. Openness—those working together freely share information with each other.

In our experience, educators who have successfully connected with a significant learning network and have benefitted from being associated with such a network exhibit these five traits themselves and connect with other educators who exhibit them as well. Finally, in an earlier book, *4 CORE Factors for School Success*, Whitaker and Zoul offered what is called our own "Top Ten Trust Traits" that great educators share in common: "be there, show you care, provide resources, communicate regularly, involve others, celebrate success, value diversity and dissent, support innovation, address underperformance, and demonstrate personal integrity" (2008, pp. 98–99).

All of the above Ten Trust Traits—with the possible exception of number nine, addressing underperformance—are ones we have written about in this book already or will write about in this and subsequent chapters. Connected educators value trust. They are highly trustworthy people and demand that those within the learning networks are also trustworthy. They rely on their colleagues near and far for various forms of support and expect those colleagues to rely on them as well. They have found that taking a chance and trusting another educator halfway around the world almost always pays dividends, resulting in a new idea, a better way to do something, access to a new resource, an opportunity to connect students from the two schools together, and most importantly, a relationship with someone they would not otherwise have met had they limited their learning network to those toiling by their sides daily in their schools. Such educators trust that the extra effort will be worth it in the long run and trust that the person they are connecting with professionally is someone with whom they can interact in a safe and open manner.

In the first chapter of this book, we suggested that becoming a connected educator starts with, logically, building a personal and professional learning network. This can actually be a bit of a scary proposition, at first, for many educators. They are not sure whether they can trust the people "following" them. They may not trust that their own tweets are actually worth sharing. They may fear that they will never be able to grow a large enough P^{2}LN to actually learn anything that will truly impact their professional lives. They may even fear the "safety" of Twitter, thinking that someone could be interacting with them with ulterior motives in mind. For connected educators who stick with this learning process, these fears eventually fade away, primarily because of the trust they sense from the connected global educational community from which their learning network is comprised. They have learned to trust that their followers, by and large, are people much like them, who are simply passionate about what they do and want to do it as well as they possibly can. They begin to trust that no one will think badly of anything they post in a tweet, in a blog, or anywhere else, whether it is a resource they are sharing, a photo they are showing about something from their school, a quote they enjoy, or an opinionated comment on a current issue in our schools. They come to trust in their network as a group of accepting, supportive, non-judgmental professionals who are there to enrich, not damage, the profession and those who serve in it. It requires a great deal of trust to "put yourself out there" in front of the entire world, sharing your photo, your biography, your opinions, your ideas, your resources, your schools and classrooms. Thankfully, we know of almost no circumstances where this trust was violated in any way within the online educational community. Moreover, once this sense of mutual respect and trust is established, the possibilities are endless in terms of what can happen to positively impact others and be positively impacted, in return.

▶ EXPECT THE BEST . . . RESPOND IN KIND

In their book *Encouraging the Heart*, a work largely about relationships in the workplace, Kouzes and Posner shared what they called their "Seven Essentials of Encouraging" (2003a, p. 15). In this framework for encouraging others, the second essential they described in detail was "Expect the Best" (p. 18). Connected educators tend to be people who both personally and professionally "expect the best" from those with whom they associate. They expect a great deal from the students they teach, the parents of these students, the colleagues working alongside them in their schools and districts, and even the members of their extended learning networks. In return, they expect just as much, if not more, from themselves. They put a great amount of time and effort into the professional relationships they establish and find that, often, this investment of time and effort is well worth it.

One way P^2LN members expect the best from each other is by calling on them whenever they need support. If, for example, one person is searching for ideas to transition to a 1:1 learning environment, he or she expects to receive assistance from the learning network to which he or she is connected. It might start with something as simple as tweeting out a call for help, asking for ideas, resources, and contacts. Often, the person will ask that members of the PLN retweet (RT) the request for assistance so that this initial plea may eventually make its way to thousands of educators across many learning networks. The PLN member who sends out the request relies on and expects at least several members of their PLN to respond to this request, actually taking time to consider it, offer help directly if they can, or send it to other colleagues asking for help if they cannot. In turn, the educator sending out the call for help fully expects to return this favor at some point in the future, likely sooner rather than later.

Another way educators expect their learning network members to be there for them is when they have a specific professional development need and they know someone in their learning network has the capability to provide expertise. Oftentimes, such educators contact a learning network member directly, via email, phone, text, or a Twitter direct message (DM) asking if the person could actually visit their school or district to lead a training session on an area of expertise in which they have had success. Connected educators tend to answer this call and provide support in some way if at all possible. We have asked several members of our learning networks to participate in professional learning events we have organized and they have always been ready and willing to lend a hand and present to our groups when called upon. Once again, the person asking for assistance in this way expects to provide reciprocal support whenever called upon.

Another way we expect our PLN colleagues to support us is through Twitter chats in which we are moderating or participating. Connected educators often moderate or guest moderate hour-long Twitter chats, described in Chapter 2. Whether they are participating in or moderating a chat, it is not at all unusual for them to ask colleagues they know with special expertise related to the chat topic to either join in the chat as a participant or even guest *host* or moderate the chat for the hour it is being conducted. Connected educators who make a difference through their PLN try to be available for such learning support opportunities whenever possible. As always, one good deed deserves another and the person being called upon to lead a chat on one occasion will often call on the person asking the favor to lead in a similar manner at some point down the road.

Another expectation we have for our PLN members, and that we hope they have for us, is simply that they are available to listen when we need an ear. Often as educators we run across a situation that arises in our classroom, in our school, in our district that strikes us as both important and urgent. It may be a situation we are facing with a student, a parent, a supervisor, or a colleague. At times, instead of turning to someone within our current organization for advice, it behooves us to seek out someone from our learning network who can offer an outside perspective into the situation. In times

> **❝**At times, instead of turning to someone within our current organization for advice, it behooves us to seek out someone from our learning network who can offer an outside perspective into the situation.**❞**

like this, it is not uncommon for us—and other members of our learning networks—to pick up a phone and call a trusted PLN colleague for support. This support typically consists of mere active listening followed, perhaps, with a suggestion for how to proceed or simply some ideas to consider. As in the cases above, the person placing such a call fully expects to be on the other end of the situation at some point and, as a result, always makes him/herself available to PLN members who need someone to help them think through a problem they are facing or an issue they are working through.

Connected educators have high expectations for everyone with whom they interact professionally—and even higher expectations for themselves. When they need assistance of any kind from a member of their learning network, they are not afraid to ask for such help and, frankly, expect to receive it. Learning networks are fluid groups and, over time, we welcome new educators to our network while others drop out. Dedicated members of personal and professional learning networks are not spending this much time in addition to the many hours they put into their regular work day merely for social purposes or to see how large their PLN can become. Instead, they are committed to this endeavor purposefully. They fully expect to get better at what they do as professionals and grow both personally and professionally by connecting with their PLN. If they find a PLN member is not contributing anything of substance or has ceased being active in the community completely, it is not uncommon to "unfollow" such members at some point so we can better attend to those members who expect a great deal from all PLN members and expect even more of themselves, in return.

▶ A PERSONAL TOUCH

A criticism we have heard from some educators who are not connected outside their local workplace and who may not fully understand all aspects of being connected is that they do not have time to waste keeping up with people they do not know online via Twitter, Facebook, Google Plus, or any other virtual platform. In our own experience—and the experiences of hundreds of other educators we have connected with outside our immediate work assignments—nothing could be further from the truth. In fact, we have found that our external learning network is every bit as important as our immediate learning network and that many parallels exist.

In a typical school, a teacher may work with, perhaps, 40 other classroom teachers. In some school districts, a principal may work with 10–20 other principals and assistant principals across the district in which they serve. A superintendent may have a few assistant superintendents with whom s/he works closely and even a local superintendents' group of neighboring superintendents who meet periodically to discuss issues they face in common. In each of these cases, two points come to mind. First, these numbers are not enough to support all the learning and skills we need to acquire. With access to such tools and knowledge so readily available to us in a connected society, it strikes us as ineffective and inefficient not to take advantage of such an opportunity. Second, we have found that our extended learning network is not unlike these more immediate learning networks in that there are some within each network whom we become closer to than others. There are some we turn to more often in both networks than others. There are some in each instance with whom we forge not only close professional relationships, but also close personal relationships. Being connected with other educators around the world in an online community of any kind does not exclude you from establishing close personal, as well as professional, bonds.

If someone follows 1,000 or more educators on Twitter, that person will obviously not become personally connected to all 1,000, even though they may, periodically, glean some insight into education from everyone they follow. We maintain that this is not unlike the regular workplace. Even if you work in a school with, say, 50 other educators, we would surmise that you are not especially close with all 50. Instead, you may have a close-knit bond with perhaps ten of these colleagues and an even tighter bond with the few who are on your hallway, or who teach the same grade or subject as you. This same ratio holds true with online PLNs. If someone follows 1,000 people on Twitter, we would venture to say that they follow 100 (or 10%) or so very closely, and of this 10%, there are perhaps around 50, or 5%, with whom they have established a very close partnership, one in which they would feel comfortable calling the other individual to ask a favor or expect to be called upon in return. In essence, the relational aspect to online PLNs is very similar to—and every bit as important as—the relational aspect within our school settings. Teachers and school administrators who are outstanding relationship builders in the workplace are also likely to excel in this area with their PLN. Similarly, those in our schools (a small percentage, to be sure) who are crummy at relationship building are not likely to be the ones on Twitter every night interacting with a following of 10,000 PLN members. Chances are, they are not all that interested in connecting with other educators in their spare time or, if they do, they quickly find that they are not establishing close relationships in this milieu either.

But for those educators who do value the professional relationships they establish in their own schools and then seek out additional professional colleagues with whom to interact, the rewards are limitless and much like those they have established in the workplace. We know of hundreds of instances in which people who have never met in person have become close personally. One PLN member offered his personal cell phone number to Jeff to give to his college-age daughter who lived 1,000 miles from home but very close to this PLN member. He said, "I'm a father, too; I get it. Tell her to call me 24/7 if she ever needs anything at all the entire time she is here." This, from someone he had never met! Todd has actually co-authored a book with someone he has never met in person and would never have known at all if not for his decision to build a PLN. Jimmy has offered his home to more than a dozen educators from around the world who have passed through his neck of the woods for one reason or another. In addition, each of us has contributed small donations of money and time to PLN members in need or causes our PLN members were supporting.

> 66 Interacting with PLN members in a largely 'virtual' manner may seem, at first, to be an impersonal way of interacting, growing, and learning. Nothing could be further from the truth. 99

Interacting with PLN members in a largely "virtual" manner may seem, at first, to be an impersonal way of interacting, growing, and learning. Nothing could be further from the truth. Everything in our jobs comes back to relationships and finding a way to make a personal connection, providing a personal touch to the people with whom we work. Our jobs are too demanding and our responsibilities too great to not take advantage of both the collegiality and the congeniality of our colleagues. Educators who are outstanding—whether they limit their professional connections to those they work alongside in person or whether they include a network of outside experts of 1,000 or more—always place relationships at the forefront and never forget the personal touch, not just the professional obligation, of the relationship.

▶ CELEBRATE GOOD TIMES

In every school we have visited that exuded a positive and productive school culture, the educators working within that school setting consciously found ways to celebrate the work they were doing, their students, their school community, and each other. Connected educators find ways to celebrate with their PLN in much the same way.

Celebrating with our learning network colleagues can take many forms. Often, these are very quick and simple things learning network members do to recognize each other and to highlight the good things that are happening within their schools or in their own careers. When something good happens at a school where a PLN member works, colleagues in the PLN are quick to tweet out these good happenings to everyone they know. When a member of the PLN receives any type of individual recognition, again, fellow learning network members are quick to highlight them publicly, letting the world know of their accomplishment. Although most PLN members focus 80% or more of their online communication on strictly professional items, there are occasions when they share personal news about something good that happened in their family or about a personal goal they recently accomplished, such as running a marathon, losing weight, completing an advanced degree, or even traveling to a bucket-list location. In all such instances, PLN colleagues are excited to share in this joy and often spread the word to their online network through a simple tweet.

In addition to these quick and easy ways to celebrate each other, PLN members who have established close relationships online ultimately try to find a way to connect in person and simply celebrate their professional friendship in a face-to-face meeting. Over the past few years, it has not been uncommon for each of us to meet up with fellow PLN members whenever we are traveling to a professional conference, another school or district, or even, at times, when traveling on a personal vacation. In doing so, we have found that we are not alone in this habit of seeking out our PLN members' company whenever we are in their vicinity. We know of hundreds of educators originally connected solely through Twitter who went on to meet together in person far from their home location to attend dinner together, attend a professional sporting event together, or present at conferences together. Such in-person celebrations speak to the power and endurance of relationships originally created online with other passionate educators around the globe.

At the national level, even the federal government in our country is jumping on the bandwagon by celebrating connected educators. The Office of Educational Technology (OET), in the Office of the Secretary of Education, provides leadership for transforming education through the power of technology, including working to help educators across the United States become more connected to each other. In 2012, they organized the first ever "Connected Educators Month," which takes place in October. To read more about this celebration of connected educators and watch an excellent five-minute video celebrating connected educators with insights into the topic from highly connected educators around the country, please visit this link, Celebrating Connected Educator Month, 2014 at http://connectededucators.org/tag/connected-educator-month-2014/ (Office of Career, Technical, and Adult Education, 2013).

▶ VALUE DIVERSITY AND DISSENT

In our list of "Top Ten Trust Traits" shared previously, the trait of valuing diversity and dissent was included as something we do if we wish to be viewed as trustworthy and something we look for in others in whom we trust. Connected educators tend to be trusting educators and part of this trust includes trusting *themselves* enough to actively seek out P²LN members who look, act, think, and speak differently than they, themselves, do. Moreover, such educators trust themselves and their P²LN members to exchange ideas and opinions that are completely honest, even when they know not everyone will agree. Valuing diversity and dissent in the composition of our P²LNs and the conversations which take place therein is a key to learning and growing within a learning network environment.

If all we do in building and expanding our network of educational colleagues is find more educators who think like we do, look like we do, and hold the exact same job title we do, we are not likely to grow and learn, which is the primary impetus for creating a PLN in the first place. Educators who have successfully made the leap into the connected environment have done so by actively seeking out educators of all backgrounds, including race, gender, socio-economic status, urban/rural settings, roles or job titles, political leanings, age/experience levels, and nations of origin. Our schools and classrooms are becoming increasingly diverse places, mirroring the greater trend in our societies overall. To the extent possible, our learning networks should reflect this diverse composition as well. As a result, many connected educators intentionally endeavor to connect with people from all walks of life. Although their network may well consist almost exclusively of people related in some way to education, you will probably note that any educator connected to a thousand or more people online likely counts within that number high school teachers, middle grade teachers, elementary school teachers, administrators, higher education professionals, parents, consultants, writers, and even politicians who have exhibited an interest in educational issues. The wider they cast their nets when seeking out learning network members to connect with and learn from, the more diverse and rich their learning will be, with perspectives from a variety of lenses represented. Although any educator with a substantial number of PLN members certainly includes among that number many who hold similar jobs and similar professional interests to their own, they know that it is important to learn opposing points of view and gain varying perspectives on issues; they seek not only those who might validate their thinking, but also those who may challenge their thinking in positive and productive ways.

> **"**If all we do in building and expanding our network of educational colleagues is find more educators who think like we do, look like we do, and hold the exact same job title we do, we are not likely to grow and learn, which is the primary impetus for creating a PLN in the first place.**"**

In addition to actively seeking to connect with a diverse collection of educators whom they can trust as fellow citizens wishing to make a difference, connected educators also strive to engage in professional discourse through public online forums that are marked by honesty, including, at times, dialogues marked by respectful disagreements, debates, and dissenting points of view. In our experience, this is actually one area in which a great deal of work remains to be done. Quite often, such conversations occur on Twitter and can become viewed as a bit of an echo chamber in which everyone participating is already connected in some way and tends to largely agree on the topic being discussed. There are even some highly connected educators who are known for not necessarily being open to opposing points of view when serious issues are up for discussion. Still, the most respected and successful connected educators find a way to welcome diverse points of views in any conversations in which they participate. They are not afraid to speak their mind openly and not afraid to respectfully rebut a fellow educator's point of view. They know that almost everyone involved in the conversation ultimately has the same goal in mind whenever they are discussing an issue that affects education, which is "What is the best course of action for the students we serve?" However, they also know that honest, reasonable, intelligent educators can have opposing—and legitimate—points of view about precisely what *is* best for kids. Very seldom do we find in our profession that we are faced with simple, black–white, yes–no, all-or-nothing situations. Ours is a world filled with gray—not just black and white—and a world comprised of not just science, but also art; as a result, we know that those with whom we interact will not always agree with our way of approaching a problem, implementing an innovation, or monitoring our schools' progress. Instead of shying away from such professional conflict, connected educators tend to embrace these occasions as opportunities for growth and honest discourse. By doing so, they honor the profession itself: by modeling how we want our students to engage in intellectual debate.

To be completely honest, we suspect that most educational PLNs as a whole are more alike than different. After all, educators who tend to go above and beyond the required amount of hours necessary to fulfill their job obligations to seek out additional avenues for professional learning tend to have much in common. It would follow, logically, that such educators who connect outside the workplace to continue growing will be similar in many ways: they will be passionate, hard-working, energetic, curious, reflective, and collaborative-minded professionals. Having said that, in our experiences, we have found many educators possessing these traits who work in distinctly different environments and who come from widely varying backgrounds; thus, we encourage you to broaden the scope of your PLN to include members with diverse backgrounds and perspectives.

As Fullan (2001) noted in the quote introducing this chapter, you cannot get anywhere without relationships. Connected educators know this as well as anyone and work to create and maintain positive and productive relationships with the people they see on a daily basis, in addition to the people they connect with on a regular basis.

FOLLOW 5, FIND 5, TAKE 5

Follow 5: These five educators from our PLN stand as models in the areas we have written about in this chapter: never forgetting that ours is a people-focused profession and nothing is more important than the relationships we create with our kids, our parents, and our colleagues. We have listed their names along with their Twitter "handles." We encourage you to follow these exemplary educators on Twitter and interact with them to enhance your life as a connected educator. Here are short insights from these experts in the field on the value of serving as a connected educator who focuses on relationships first:

1. *Rick Wormeli (@RickWormeli)*. Education writer and consultant, Herndon, Virginia. Rick is a key contributor to Standards-Based Learning Chat on Twitter (#sblchat), Wednesdays, 8:00–9:00 CST. According to Wormeli,

Faculties in which the majority participate in the national conversations of their fields and profession are much more successful with new building initiatives and instructional growth. These faculties have larger, healthier perspectives, and they have a much wider repertoire of resources upon which to draw as they face new challenges. They realize they are not alone in their efforts, and in turn, this inspires courageous acts of pedagogy. Seriously, we cannot be brave or creative with what we do not have. Twitter and online communities of discussion facilitate all these positives readily, 24/7. We get access to the wealth of insight, practicality, and successful issue wrangling on any subject from respected colleagues, even teacher/principal heroes, from around the world, and it's all free. What a blazing comet of education fire and wisdom I would have been today if I only had Twitter and similar communities back when I first started studying teaching in the late 70s! Think of today's students whose teachers take every opportunity to participate in these communities—Wow, what learning, what achievement!

2. *Jennie Magiera (@MsMagiera)*. Digital Learning Coordinator, Chicago, Illinois. Jennie is a regular contributor to #mathchat and #edchat and blogs at www.teachinglikeits2999.com. According to Magiera,

Being connected is more than a follow on Twitter or joining an online forum. It's being brave enough to ask questions, share ideas and wonder aloud with others. I value the connections I make both face to face and virtually not only for the ideas I glean but also the action we take following the connection. The ability to learn, try, fail, iterate and try again with colleagues can have an incredibly positive impact on our practice.

3. *Dennis Schug (@DJrSchug)*. Middle School Principal, Long Island, New York. Dennis is a regular participant in the following Twitter chats: #IAedchat, #aledchat, #arkedchat, #colchat, #nyedchat, #ptchat, and #satchat. According to Schug,

Today, every educator must be courageous in rising to the challenge of pursuing excellence as 21st Century Learning Leaders. We now have an unprecedented obligation to support, motivate, and invest in our students, our colleagues, our communities, and in one another, in ways that must transcend classroom walls. There is no substitute for face-to-face interactions and the role personal relationships play in inspiring and challenging our professional growth, but being receptive to social media communities as avenues for transparent connections makes the world smaller, refines resources, and expands potential for all Learning Leaders. Using social media removes walls and eliminates time constraints to reveal opportunities for personalized learning that keeps focus on those who matter most: our students.

4. *Tara Copeman (@copers)*. Assistant Principal; Edmonton, Alberta. Tara regularly participates in #edchat, #edtech, #techchat, #abed, and #atplc. According to Copeman,

My greatest love about being connected is the ability to create and maintain collegial relationships across time and space. Whether creating new connections online then the thrill of meeting in real life, or meeting in-person at an event and being able to collaborate well beyond your conference, Twitter becomes a low-risk forum to extend your network of experts. It also allows you to tap the shoulders of experts without feeling like you are putting them out—everyone has time for a response in 140 characters! It is through our humanity that we connect to others who share our passions in order to exchange ideas and resources so that we both are enriched in the process.

5. *John Wink (@JohnWink90)*. Director of Curriculum, Instruction, and Assessment, Tatum Independent School District in Tatum, Texas. John regularly participates in #satchat, #IAedchat, #edchat, #wischat, and #txeduchat. According to Wink,

Participating in chats and striving to model connected learning is not staff development; it is thought development. Learning with others through social media helps simplify the complexities in education. By connecting with educators across the world at any time of day, I lead my own learning in a personalized fashion. Thanks to my PLN of virtual colleagues, my knowledge and leadership have increased exponentially.

Find 5: We have found these five online resources to be particularly useful in reflecting on the power of relationships, particularly with members of your PLN. These are links to resources that we have learned about via our own PLN and that we have used ourselves to improve some aspect of our job performance or expand our thinking in this important area:

1. Relationships: Who Needs Them? by Tom Whitby (@tomwhitby) at http://edupln.ning.com/profiles/blogs/relationships-who-needs-them.
2. Developing Strong Relationships with Your PLN by Shelly Terrell (@shellterell) at http://shellyterrell.com/2009/08/03/developing-strong-relationships-with-your-pln/.
3. You Can't be a Great Leader Without Trust. Here's How You Build It by David Horsager at http://www.forbes.com/sites/forbesleadershipforum/2012/10/24/you-cant-be-a-great-leader-without-trust-heres-how-you-build-it/
4. What is a PLN? Why Do I Need One? by Jordan Catapano (@BuffEnglish) at http://www.teachhub.com/what-pln-why-do-i-need-one.
5. Relationships Matter by Sean Slade (@SladeSean) at http://www.huffingtonpost.com/sean-slade/relationships-matter_b_1110001.html.

Take 5: We conclude each chapter by recommending five action steps you can take to get started or continue on your path as a connected educator. Here are five steps we suggest you take to make the most of your relationships with your learning network colleagues:

1. In this chapter, we discussed the importance of diversity and dissent within your PLN. Take stock of who is currently in your PLN and note any groups you feel are underrepresented. Make it a

point to add 10–20 members who will extend the diversity of your learning network.

2. How trustworthy are you? Take a free, online quiz to determine your level of trustworthiness. This online assessment consists of 20 questions and takes just a few minutes to complete. It scores your answers, compares you to the average score, and offers additional suggestions based on your responses. Although free, it does require an email address to complete: http://trustsuite.trustedadvisor.com/.

3. Actively seek out an opportunity to tweet an opinion that conflicts with another educator's point of view. Obviously, please do so in a respectful, dignified manner; however, be honest, too, sharing your sincere opinion and why you feel that way. Note any responses you receive in return. Make an effort to agree and support your PLN when your views align with theirs. At the same time, do not be afraid to speak your mind—even when this may contradict others with whom you are interacting.

4. Find something that someone is sharing on Twitter as a personal or professional accomplishment. Take time to tweet out a response, congratulating them. Take time also to retweet the original post. Consider sending a handwritten note to the mailing address of the person, adding an even more personal touch to the recognition.

5. Ask your PLN for help with an issue you are facing. In addition to sending out a tweet asking for help and asking them to retweet the request, consider calling three of your most trusted PLN members, to hear—not just read in 140 characters—their advice, suggestions, ideas. Listen actively to what they say, thank them, and offer to return the favor when they need a willing ear.

Model the Way

*Who you are speaks so loudly I can't hear what
you are saying.*

Ralph Waldo Emerson

Everyone has the capacity to lead, but every effective educator knows that no matter how willing and able they are to lead the way, they cannot do it alone; they must work in a way that not only encourages others to follow but also creates more opportunities for others to lead. They are committed to modeling behaviors and attitudes which contribute positively to the culture of their school community or education in general with the belief that any individual can make a significant impact upon an organization. The work that is expected in our schools today from those who work there to serve students, parents, and the community requires more of a connected leadership approach that is transparent and based on a foundation of trust. Moreover, it requires an approach that is purposeful and values not only each member of the organization itself—from every student to every teacher—but also every stakeholder outside the organization, including parents, community members, and other connected educators.

Connected learners model the way for others. They look around and know the shadow they are casting. They know they cannot ask students and colleagues to do what they are not willing to do themselves. Whether they work in a classroom or

> **❝**Connected learners model the way for others. . . . They know they cannot ask students and colleagues to do what they are not willing to do themselves.**❞**

in the principal's office, they model a collaborative culture in which every member of the team feels inspired to reach outside their comfort zone and take a risk. They are open and forthcoming with their thoughts and words. We know their passions, what they believe in, and what they stand for by the actions they take and the practices they model on a daily basis. Their focus remains strictly on the impact these actions and practices have on their students or team members, rather than how they impact them personally. Connected learners recognize that the success of any classroom, program, school, or school community is based on the premise that with the right mindset we can accomplish anything and that we must model not only the right mindset but also the corresponding behaviors and attitudes to reap the most positive cultural shifts. Connected educators know—like Emerson so wisely pointed out many years ago—that our actions speak much louder than our words and that to positively impact others we must model the way.

▶ HOW WE RESPOND IS OUR CHOICE

Modeling the way is not just a catchphrase, but a conduit to unlimited possibilities for connected learners everywhere to strengthen their school cultures by setting a positive example. In their best selling book, Kouzes and Posner identified what they termed "five exemplary leadership practices," the first of which they called "Model the Way" (2003b, p. 41). In our visits to hundreds of schools and thousands of classrooms within these schools, we have found that the very best teachers model for students what they, in turn, expect from them. Similarly, the best school leaders with whom we have worked intentionally model the attitudes, behaviors, and commitments they expect from the teachers they serve. By modeling the way, teachers and leaders encourage those they teach and lead to behave according to shared values so that they can achieve a shared vision for excellence. Watching what you say, leading by example, making sure your actions align with how you act, and reinforcing the behaviors you want to see are all important aspects of modeling the way. Leadership in our schools and in our classrooms is based on relationships that must be nurtured. Connected educators model these relationship skills with the students they teach and the colleagues with whom they interact.

Keep in mind that we operate under the premise that teachers are leaders and leaders are teachers. Likewise, connected *teachers* are connected *leaders* and vice versa. Often, once an educator in a school or district begins realizing the power and encouragement that comes from being connected to a supportive PLN, they set a goal to enlist others in the schools and districts they serve to become connected with a PLN as well. To do so, they make sure to model the way, placing a premium on cultivating relationships with both their building teams as well as their extended network of colleagues, as was shared in the previous chapter. They value the learning and personal reflection that come from these relationships and give of their time and energy to nurture them. They are constantly sharing and engaging in professional dialogue with their peers and supervisors while bringing a positive voice to their work environment on a daily basis. Many connected educators with whom we have interacted believe fervently that one person can make a difference in the lives of others and they operate under a philosophy of "no blame, no fault . . . but, also, no excuses" when things do not go as planned. If they are faced with a difficult problem, they focus not on blame, fault, or excuses, but on brainstorming specific solutions designed to address the problem. When it comes to modeling the way for colleagues who may be interested in connecting with others, they know that the support they provide cannot be limited to a one-time event. Getting started as a connected educator is much like anything else worth doing: it takes time and effort on the front end.

When first getting started as a connected educator—or, on a larger scale, as a connected school community—problems will arise. One such problem that is sure to arise is students misusing social media in some way that is harmful to themselves, other students, or the school in general. How we respond when such things occur can determine whether it happens more or less frequently in the future. To clarify this point let us share an example that we have observed in schools that do not support or embrace connected learning.

Many school leaders across the country adopt a *lock and block* approach when it comes to the use in school of social media tools such as Facebook, YouTube, and Twitter. They often do so with the best intentions, of course; at the same time, they often do so by assuming the worst about people and treating all people within the school as if they were bad, instead of taking the opposite approach and treating everyone within the school as if they were good—in other words, expecting students and staff to do what is right, not wrong. They often hide behind the following hypothetical to make their decisions: "What if. . .?" *What if* a student links to an inappropriate website? *What if* a student tweets something inappropriate about another student or staff member? *What if* a student spends all of their time searching Facebook instead of doing their classwork? *What if* they break into the school's network?

The truth is that these things are going to happen. Your response dictates how you overcome these concerns. Too often our response is to want to take away the tools and resources that we believe are the root cause of these behaviors, as was the case in the Los Angeles Unified School District in September of 2013 when students at Roosevelt High School figured out a way to hack the security system so they could use their school-issued iPads without school filtering restrictions (Silva, 2013). Only one week after being issued the iPads, students could access personal Facebook accounts and surf the web for inappropriate sites. When school officials discovered the security breach, their first response was to stop distribution of iPads to other students in the district. We realize that problems arise as technology becomes increasingly available in our schools. We also realize that as educators, we should treat such instances as teachable moments. Certainly, students should be held accountable for conduct that is detrimental to them or others. The answer is not, however, to take away tools that we think will help them become more prepared for college and careers. Just as we should not take a textbook away from a student who defaces it, we cannot and must not respond by taking away technology from students who misuse it.

The concern with the scenario above is that all students were ultimately denied access to a digital tool because of the actions of a few, in this case, approximately three hundred out of hundreds of thousands of students enrolled in the district. Connected school leaders recognize that living in a connected world comes with challenges, but rather than hide from those challenges, they embrace them. They view these experiences as learning opportunities and as a way to build relationships with students they previously may not have known. They model a mindset that focuses on teaching, rather than punishment, by reaching out to students to understand why they did what they did and then work together to come up with an alternative solution. Ultimately, connected educators operate under a 95/5 rule, which means they do not make decisions based on the fear of what 5% of the population might do (which usually means challenging authority or school policies) but on the knowledge of what is best for the other 95% who rarely, if ever, break school rules.

In Chapter 3, we discussed the pride and value many connected leaders find in sharing the story of their schools. They focus on the importance of bringing their school community closer together by trusting their students and staff with an open access mindset, allowing them to brand their school through the use of readily available social media tools. They take every opportunity to integrate a curriculum that focuses on digital leadership and citizenship with students in the school in order to protect a student's digital profile. They create school hashtags and highlight student and staff tweets on video screens throughout the school. They display Twitter feeds on large projector screens in auditoriums during student assemblies to gather feedback and give students a voice in their school. They use backchannels like Today's Meet (see www.todaysmeet.com) during faculty meetings to gather questions and encourage dialogue and discussion. When asked who monitors the tweets and pictures that are placed on display to make sure they are appropriate, the common response from connected educators is the students, staff, and school community monitor themselves. And when an issue does occur, they hold students accountable by teaching the importance of protecting their digital footprint, rather than focusing on punishing the student. Ultimately, this approach leads to fewer and fewer incidents of concerns associated with technology and social media in our schools. Within a school culture that models and expects every member of the school community to look out for one another and values the voice of each member of that community, the mindset they operate under is: what we model is largely what we get. There are times, despite our very best efforts at modeling ourselves on what we expect from others, when we will be disappointed and will be faced with students behaving inappropriately. When these incidents occur, how we respond as connected educators is our choice and ours alone. The choice we make sets the stage for future patterns of behavior. If we choose to respond with a blanket approach, treating all students with suspicion and distrust, we are likely to encourage more of the same. If, on the other hand, we choose to respond by treating all students as if they were good and modeling the way, eventually we establish a culture in which more and more students follow the way we are modeling.

> **❝** If . . . we choose to respond by treating all students as if they were good and modeling the way, eventually we establish a culture in which more and more students follow the way we are modeling. **❞**

▶ HOW WE INSPIRE IS OUR CHOICE

How we respond when things do not go the way we plan is our choice. How we inspire is our choice, too. Successful educators believe in the notion that success breeds success, but more importantly, they realize that personal growth is a critical factor in ongoing and enduring success. What made us successful in the past may not keep us successful in the future, but if we are continuously learning and growing, we learn how to succeed in a society that is ever-changing. Connected educators model the way in this area by pursuing learning opportunities in a variety of ways and working to inspire others to behave likewise. They recognize that change is, rather ironically, here to stay. Many educators understand that being a member of a connected community that is largely online can be a complex undertaking and that staying the course is not without its challenges. Most who are able to persevere have a passion for teaching and learning and creating environments in which great things can happen. Learning spaces that are caring, open, and engaging spaces tend to promote innovation and

> **❝** What made us successful in the past may not keep us successful in the future, but if we are continuously learning and growing, we learn how to succeed in a society that is ever-changing. **❞**

creativity, traits we hope to instill within the students who populate them. Connected educators inspire their students and colleagues by recognizing every success begins with failure. They model through their actions that it is acceptable to fail and that risk-taking is encouraged.

Today's schools cannot have a one-size-fits-all approach to getting students and adults to perform at high levels. Therefore, connected leaders and teachers together must find ways to model the importance of leading and learning with a sense of passion, purpose, and pride. Teachers are fulfilled when they believe the work they are doing makes a difference in the lives of the students they teach. Students also want to have a more far-reaching influence by taking on social issues within their community and across the globe. They want to fight for causes that are significant and have a greater impact on the world they will one day lead.

One such connected young student whom we have gotten to know through our PLN is Zak Malamed (@zakmal), who is a junior at the University of Maryland in College Park, Maryland. Two years ago, Zak founded #stuvoice, an online Twitter chat for students, as a platform where students could express their own views regarding educational topics affecting them in this country. Zak moderates #stuvoice each Monday evening at 8:30 EST. According to Malamed,

> Every student needs to take ownership over the direction of their own life. Too often we try to place students in leadership positions but this leads to them not leading for themselves, but, instead, following a trajectory that others have set out for them. This is not really true student voice. We ask students to lead this event or lead this club, but we don't allow them to choose the route the organization or how the learning experience should go, rather it is already pre-determined for them. This is not real world, valuable, experience. So we set out as an organization and the movement of student voice to create a platform for students to be voices for themselves. We don't tell students what issues they should be advocating for or what issues should be important to them. Instead, Student Voice gives them the platform to decide for themselves so together they can make change. We

believe we have made this integration of student voice more practical for us to choose who we want to be rather than be told what by others (adults) who we should be. We want to be independent and own our own learning through our early years. We want a more open learning model and this is why we believe Student Voice is so important and how it is helping transform education as a whole.

As connected educators, we strive to inspire our students to be lifelong learners who are invested in their own education. Zak is an example of one such student who, in turn, is inspiring other students around the world to find their own voice and inspiration.

Teachers also need to feel empowered to believe their voice matters and that they have the autonomy and flexibility to make decisions regarding how they deliver curriculum, instruction, and assessments to their students. Our very best educators believe in a guaranteed and viable curriculum for all students as a matter of fairness and equal access. Connected educators believe in this, too, though they also believe in allowing for autonomy in how we get students from where they are to where they need to get to, so that they display mastery of agreed-upon performance standards. They want to feel supported and trust that these decisions to engage students in more authentic real-world learning experiences will not be held against them by administrators who insist on one instructional style for all. Just as it is the case that we must personalize learning for individual students, we must also allow for personalized teaching and learning for our teachers. With an ever-increasing emphasis being placed on standardized test scores in school districts across the country and with teachers being held increasingly accountable for their students' performance on such tests, this is a legitimate concern in some school communities. Connected educators inspire those they teach and lead to find ways that work best for them. Mark Pisel (@mpise12), a business teacher in Iowa, shared the following insights about how he inspires students to learn:

My philosophy has always been to point students in the right direction and then get out of their way. I have found that students really enjoy going out and discovering information and trying to learn through trial and error rather than me just telling them exactly what to do all of the time. I want them to have their own experience that is unique and personal. Watching my students' progress has been fun. We are connecting with students and schools all over the world through Twitter and student blogs. Social media has allowed our learning to go to a higher level and the interactions we have had with other students from countries as far away as Saudi Arabia has been inspiring. We are now looking at ways to crowdsource our work and keep the students engaged in their learning. I really appreciate how our administration supports our teaching. Every time we come to them with an idea we never hear, "Oh, we can't do that here" or "That will never work." Instead, what we get is, "How can we help you make this happen?" And that mindset is not only refreshing, but inspiring, and makes us want to go out and do more for our students and our school.

Students and teachers want leaders who pay attention to them and who genuinely care about them. They want more than just to be told what to do. They want objective feedback and coaching. They want partners who listen to them and mentor them, who inspire their performance. Connected leaders adhere to a mantra that says, "Don't tell me why it can't work; instead, let's work together to find a way to make it happen." Students and teachers want to know that their ideas are valued and supported rather than have the lid put on them. Connected leaders recognize this and model the way accordingly, creating a culture in which they choose to inspire the teachers they serve with the expectation that these teachers, in turn, inspire their students in a like manner.

▶ HOW WE COLLABORATE IS OUR CHOICE

Connected educators recognize and understand the value of cultivating a collaborative culture that supports and develops teachers and administrators in their pursuit of personal and professional growth. As leaders, it is our responsibility to cultivate a school culture where excellence is the foundation of all that we expect and do. As teachers, it is our responsibility to cultivate a classroom culture that does the same. We must constantly model the importance of focusing on both individual needs as well as the needs of our teams by fostering an environment that encourages a community of leaders coming together, where everyone's talents are appreciated and valued and the focus is placed on advancing the students and school community they serve. Model teams incorporate three habits into their daily work: they dream big, get stuff done, and know how to have fun!

Connected leaders work diligently to provide meaningful, engaging, and collaborative learning experiences for their staff as part of their professional development by encouraging and supporting them to take ownership of their own learning and growth. They do this through a variety of methods, but they operate under the notion that the best experts exist among their own team. They utilize the talents of their own teaching staff when working together to plan building wide professional development that is relevant and engaging. In many instances, the formats that are created for professional learning are teacher-led formats where teachers set the agendas and determine the topics for discussion using an informal, grassroots model similar to Edcamps as described in Chapter 2. Other examples of ideas that connected educators have initiated in order to give teachers a greater voice and bring about a sense of ownership of their professional growth include site visits to local businesses to learn firsthand what skills are required in the workplace, site visits to other schools to see what is working well elsewhere, and teacher and school exchanges that foster a stronger PLN. Connected educators are also creating student and staff blogs as a tool for teaching, sharing, learning, and growing as a collaborative team. In connected schools, it is no longer an option for educators to work in isolation.

The Katy Independent School District (ISD), located in the Houston Metropolitan area, has been focusing on a more collaborative model for professional development for several years. Based on the work by Fullan (2014), Dr. Christine Caskey, Chief Academic Officer and Elisa Farris, Director of Professional Learning, have been working on a more systemic approach through what Fullan described as "Living

Laboratories." According to Caskey and Farris, the Katy ISD is bringing about a sense of *togetherness* by being more purposeful in how they structure their time together so that their work becomes more meaningful. These collaborative meetings, which they now refer to as "Co-Labs," are designed to develop leadership capacity. The intent is to ensure that each leader is no longer working in isolation solely focused on making their campus stronger, but has a vested interest in the entire district being great. As Farris stated,

> This time that we set aside together each month needs to be a time together where we roll up our sleeves, where we experiment, where we problem solve and talk through the challenges we are facing. And when things fail, as they are bound to do, we work through to find solutions together. We are committed to making the work and experience richer for all of us. By doing so, we will all be more successful as an entire organization.
>
> (C. Caskey and E. Farris, personal
> communication, July 25, 2014)

We must expect our students, teachers, families, and community members to come together to take part in global conversations if we expect to influence change at a greater scale. The best way to make these expectations a reality is to model them ourselves through our daily actions, behaviors, words, and commitments. It is no longer about technology transforming education; rather, it is about our pedagogy transforming our students' learning, a pedagogy that is based on what we collaboratively determine is best for students entering a connected workplace and connected world.

Connected educators believe that the key to making this transformational change lies in their ability to take the *pockets of excellence* that exist within the organizations they serve and replicating these pockets on a larger scale, connecting those who are having success in one area with others in the school or district hoping to achieve similar results. Over time, the roles reverse and the person who learns today leads someone else tomorrow, with the ultimate goal being a collaborative culture in which we all learn from each other, we all teach each other, and we all lead each other, moving from "pockets of excellence" to entire "networks of excellence," networks made up of individual team members, each of whom understands that the success of the entire organization lies in their willingness to abandon their silos and work together as one cohesive team. Connected educators leading in these ways recognize this and model the way for others by operating under the mindset of "what we model is what we get."

FOLLOW 5, FIND 5, TAKE 5

Follow 5: These five educators from our PLN stand as models in the area we have written about in this chapter: understanding that what we model is what we get. We have listed their names along with their Twitter "handles." We encourage you to follow these exemplary educators on Twitter and interact with them to enhance your life as a connected educator. Here are short insights from these experts in the field on the importance of modeling the way.

1. *Brad Currie (@bradmcurrie)*. K-8 Supervisor of Instruction/ Middle School Vice Principal in New Jersey. Brad is the co-founder and co-moderator of #satchat, a chat for current and emerging school leaders that takes place every Saturday morning at 7:30 a.m. EST. According to Currie,

Being an educator in the connected era provides an opportunity to establish relationships with some of the best minds in the education industry on a worldwide scale. For me it has been a game-changer in terms of the access I have to thought leaders and innovators who share best practice ideas and resources on a daily basis. The more people share on social media platforms such as Twitter, the better chance this will trickle down to our classrooms and impact student success. Connecting with like-minded individuals on various social media platforms has allowed me to grow in ways once thought unimaginable. It is no longer an option for educators to remain disconnected from all that is happening in the virtual world around. Social media has provided educators with a vehicle to transcend how they grow professionally and, ultimately, how they will promote the success of all students.

2. *Dr. Joe Clark (@DrJoeClark)*. Superintendent, Nordonia Hills City Schools, Northfield, Ohio. Dr. Clark is co-moderator of #ptchat, a forum for parents and teacher partnerships. According to Clark,

I try to model the expectations I have for all educators in our district through my presence on Twitter, which I use to promote school events, brag about teachers and students, and share educational, inspirational, or leadership posts or news. I also try to model the way for others by blogging regularly (http://drjoeclarkblog.wordpress.com/). I encourage all superintendents to get involved with Twitter and blogging as two ways to model lifelong learning for others. Start an account, post some district news, follow Twitter all-stars, and follow some chats. Get your feet wet and soon you'll be immersed in all Twitter and blogging have to offer.

3. *John Carver (@JohnCCarver)*. Superintendent, Howard-Winneshiek Community School District. John regularly follows #2020howardwinn, #edchat, #satchat, #IAedchat, #satchathack, and #vanmeter on Twitter. According to Carver,

We are at a "printing press" moment in the history of mankind. Digital devices and connections to the internet are transforming teaching and learning. School leaders must model the way by embracing the changes we face and showing others how crucial it is that leaders/learners are always growing, sharing, and sharpening their thinking, connecting with educational change agents globally and participating in the global education conversation.

4. *Amber Teamann (@8amber8)*. Assistant Principal, Watkins Elementary School, Wylie, Texas. Amber is the moderator of #tichat. According to Teamann,

Twitter is a tool that should be personalized to fit your needs. Not comfortable sharing? Lurk, learn, then lead! I am able to share with my colleagues relevant and timely resources to help them grow in addition to maintaining my mantra that the smartest person in the room is the room. I want my "room" to model being lifelong learners!

5. *Dominique Dynes (@dominiquedynes)*. Dominique is a sixth grade social studies teacher in Guadalajara, Mexico. She is also a Google Certified Teacher. Dominique is the founder and co-moderator of #mexedchat, which takes place on the second and fourth Monday of each month from 9 to 10 p.m. CST. According to Dynes,

Twitter changed my life as a teacher by allowing me to get connected with educators around the world. I often hear teachers say that our jobs can be very isolating and too overwhelming to find time for professional growth. Twitter chats are a great way to get motivated about what's happening in education and to constantly learn with peers all over the globe. The educators I've met on Twitter have really changed my vision of global collaboration and daily encourage me to never stop growing. As a founder of #mexedchat, one of the first bilingual ed chats on Twitter, it has been inspiring to feel the passion for what is going on in our schools in Latin America while we connect with one another each month.

Find 5: We have found these five online resources to be particularly useful in reflecting on the power of modeling, particularly with students and staff. These are links to resources that we have learned about via our own PLN and that we have used ourselves to improve some aspect of our job performance or expand our thinking in this important area:

1. Don't Be The Lid, at https://www.youtube.com/watch?v=p7Ljg xoh9ic.
2. Supporting the Teacher Maker Movement—8 Ways to Support Teachers, at http://www.edutopia.org/blog/supporting-teacher-maker-movement-heather-wolpert-gawron.
3. Genius Hour via Chris Kesler at https://www.youtube.com/watch?v=NMFQUtHsWhc.
4. Why Should People Follow You? by Jim Kouzes at https://www.youtube.com/watch?v=nhsvQ7xuBf0.
5. Four Things I Will Do Differently This School Year by Amy Ridle-huber Kingsley at http://blogs.kqed.org/education/2014/08/29/four-things-ill-do-differently-this-school-year/.

Take 5: We conclude each chapter by recommending five action steps you can take to get started or continue on your path as a connected educator. Here are five steps we suggest you take to ensure you are constantly modeling how you expect others to behave and placing a premium on inspiring others inside and outside your organization.

1. Write down five members of your P^2LN and write them a personal thankyou letter. Share with them how being connected to them has influenced you as a person and educator.
2. RSVP: Raising Student Voice and Participation. Organize your own student leadership school chapter, sponsored by NASSP. Check out the blog post link: A Student's Perspective at http://nasspblogs.org/ignite/2013/11/05/rsvp-a-students-perspective/.
3. Make a commitment to promote and advocate for Open Learning Spaces in your school so students can access social media tools such as Facebook, Twitter, YouTube, and other resources. Create and showcase your school Twitter accounts via hashtags on television monitors throughout the building.
4. If you are serving as a principal or in another school leadership role, create a system to inspire "Genius Hour" teaching and learning activities amongst your staff by covering classes for teachers in order to give them planning time to stretch their creativity and innovation.
5. Be a model by demonstrating risk-taking. Demonstrate that we can all learn from one another, by presenting an instructional practice at a staff meeting, leading a session during a professional development day at your school, facilitating a session at an Edcamp, or submitting a proposal to present at a state, regional, or national conference. Be the change you wish to see.

Key Connector 8

Know When to Unplug

I find it refreshing to unplug from it for a while. You kind of forget how deeply you get embedded in it.

Will Wright

Will Wright is an American video game designer whose greatest success to date comes from being the original designer for *The Sims*, a life simulation video game series. It is one of the most successful video game series of all time. The game spawned multiple sequels and expansions, and Wright has earned many awards for his work. Although Wright has obviously spent a great deal of his life "plugged in" to technology of various types, it is equally clear he values time away from such activities and sees the benefits of unplugging. Like Wright, perhaps, connected educators may at times find themselves getting too deeply embedded in the technology that accompanies the role. Almost all educators we know who are passionately committed to connecting with others around the world spend a great deal of time outside of their regular work hours pursuing this professional passion. However, these educators also know the importance of a work–life balance and intentionally make time to unplug and explore other outlets for connecting with friends, family members, and themselves that are totally unrelated to education or social media. Ironically, in many cases it seems as if these educators have more, not less, time to spend on pursuits outside of education and never forget that there is much more to life than working long hours each day only to go home and connect virtually with others to continue discussing professional matters.

Nearly all educators we know work extremely long hours. During the school year, many of these educators spend ten or more hours a day at their schools or offices only to go home in the evening to grade papers, plan lessons, prepare for meetings and professional learning events, or connect online with other educators to continue their learning and planning collaboratively. Teaching in and leading our schools are demanding jobs that become more, not less, consuming with each passing year. With all the demands placed upon educators in today's society, it is necessary that we schedule time for unplugging and for finding ways to connect with others in a manner unrelated to digital formats.

Studies reinforce our belief that we are in danger of spending too much time plugged in and that the results of such connectivity can hamper, rather than benefit, not only our work, but also our health. One recent study showed that smartphone users check their devices an average of 150 times during a waking day of 16 hours (Roberts & Pirog, 2012). In another study by Smith (2012), 84% of cell phone users claim they could not go a single day without their device and 67% of cell phone owners check their phone for messages, alerts, or calls—even when they do not notice their phone ringing or vibrating. The average American spends over six days each month watching traditional television, and over 30 hours each month connected to the Internet (Perez, 2013). For many people, connecting via one device is not enough: up to "88% of consumers in the United States connect via their smartphone while watching television" (Cocotas, 2013, para. 1).

The results of so much time spent plugged in to various forms of electronic devices can be harmful. According to one study, people who are regularly plugged in can have difficulty tuning out the irrelevant information facing them (Richtel, 2010). In another study from the United Kingdom, over 50% of those studied reported that social media had an overall negative impact on their lives, contributing to low self-esteem, worse sleep patterns, and anxiety (Fitzgerald, 2012). Technology use before going to sleep can be problematic because screens emit a blue wavelength of light that tricks the brain into thinking it is time to be alert, thereby delaying the natural release of the sleep-aiding hormone melatonin. The National Sleep Foundation found that "95% use a screen of some type in the hour before bed and that such usage can have a deleterious impact upon our sleep" (National Sleep Foundation, 2011, para. 4). Finally, too much connectivity can be harmful to us physically. Sitting too much in general (which we are most likely doing the majority of the time spent while connected to a device) is not healthy and poor posture can lead to a variety of ailments.

So, although we are staunch advocates for serving as connected educators and have seen firsthand how being connected with thousands of other educators can help us learn and grow professionally and personally, we also realize that balance in our lives is important and that if we are not careful, we can find ourselves spending too much time being connected online and not enough time connecting with our friends, family, nature, and our physical, emotional, and mental health. Successful educators are keenly aware of the dangers associated with working too many hours and spending too much time connected via devices and, as a result, commit to spending their time away from their workplace in a variety of ways, including time set aside for unplugging.

> 66 Successful educators are keenly aware of the dangers associated with working too many hours and spending too much time connected via devices and, as a result, commit to spending their time away from their workplace in a variety of ways, including time set aside for unplugging. 99

▶ PLAN TO UNPLUG

In order to ensure that they do not fall into the all-too-easy trap of becoming overly plugged in, successful connected educators act intentionally to fill their days with routines designed to include activities totally unrelated to technology, social media, and screen time. They set a standard for themselves in terms of when and how often they are connected to others via any type of device; they intentionally plan for chunks of time in their personal and professional lives when they focus on pursuits unrelated to connected learning. These chunks of time can vary in any number of ways and can range from brief respites of mere minutes to longer technology cleanses lasting a day or more. Just

> 66 Being connected can become too much of a good thing and it is necessary to guard against relying too much on digital connectivity as a way of life. 99

as the times we spend away from technology can vary from user to user, the outlets we find to engage in outside of connected education can also vary greatly from person to person depending upon their interests and passions. Although the ways and times in which connected educators find to unplug vary widely, one thing is certain: being connected can become too much of a good thing and it is necessary to guard against relying too much on digital connectivity as a way of life.

Whitaker (2004) wrote that in great teachers' classrooms, very little happens at random. Instead, great teachers have a plan and a purpose for everything they do. The same holds true for connected educators. To guard against spending too much time plugged in, they intentionally plan for time away from connectivity and their professional responsibilities in general. We realize that this sounds so simple and self-evident, yet we also know just how important it is. If we do not *intentionally* plan to unplug, there is a good chance we will not *find* the time to do so. We cannot stress enough the importance of *making* time to build unplugging opportunities into your regular routines. Some connected educators with whom we have worked plan this time daily with activities interspersed throughout the day set aside as opportunities to unplug. Some focus on setting aside this time in the morning as a way to start the day, at meal times, at the end of the work day, or during the final two waking hours before going to sleep. Still others set aside the majority or totality of their weekend time for pursuits other than those related to their PLN. However this time looks and whenever it occurs, the important fact is that it *does* occur, allowing them to focus, de-stress, and maintain a healthy balance between being connected versus being unplugged.

As discussed throughout this book, the possibilities for connecting with educators around world in order to grow and learn professionally are almost limitless. The possibilities for unplugging are, perhaps, even more endless depending on personal interests, locations, and family responsibilities. Having said that, we have found three simple ways that connected educators seem to have in common in terms of unplugging options: exercise, reading, and, somewhat ironically, solitude.

Exercise Obviously, not every person in the world has the capability or inclination to be an exercise fanatic and not every connected educator is either. Still, we have found that the vast majority of connected educators with whom we have worked spend some amount of time engaging their bodies physically in much the same way they engage their minds mentally as a way to achieve a healthy and balanced lifestyle. Make no mistake about it: sometimes this physical activity can be as simple as taking a walk outside, enjoying a low-key bike ride in the neighborhood, strolling along a beach, or even periodic stretch breaks away in which they stand up to get away from their desks and move about the school hallways. We know several colleagues who even work at stand-up desks as a way to combat too much seat time while connecting and working. Of course, many others we know are extremely active physically, running marathons, competing in triathlons, engaging in daily weight-room sessions, enrolling in yoga classes, playing tennis or softball, or hiking. The way in which connected educators engage in physical activity can and does vary greatly depending on a variety of factors, but most realize that our work as connected educators is largely characterized by sitting in place and long stretches of physical inactivity and, as a result, consciously find ways to stay physically, as well as mentally, engaged. Making time to engage their bodies physically to some extent is one way that connected educators intentionally unplug.

Reading The very best educators we know read a great deal. The reading they do includes both professional reading and pleasure reading. They stay abreast of current events around the world as well as current events and practices in their job-specific area, whether they are school principals or high school English teachers. In recent years, the options for accessing reading materials have increased rather dramatically. We can read on our computers, on our phones, and on a variety of tablets. The type of material we are reading has also changed. Many educators spend a great deal of time reading blog posts written by other educators and a variety of articles shared online by members of their learning network. Once again, the following does not hold true of absolutely every great connected educator we know, but we have found that most enjoy—and, therefore, still prioritize—reading books, magazines, and newspapers offline, in traditional print formats. Many connected educators we know still start their day by quietly reading a daily newspaper while enjoying a cup of coffee. Others insist that the best part of their learning remains the 15–20 minutes spent reading a print copy of a book they keep at their bedside before they go to sleep each evening. Still others talk about the reading they do in their classrooms alongside their students who are also reading independently. Many subscribe to professional journals or general magazines, which they look forward to reading each week or month. In the same way that physical activity can vary widely according to the interests and capabilities of the specific educator, reading styles can also vary widely depending on the consumer of the reading. We have found, however, that connected educators tend not to limit their reading material solely to online text and they tend to read not only via electronic tools such as computers and tablets, but also by accessing traditional print resources. Although reading is an activity requiring intellectual engagement, when done so independently, quietly, and with traditional print material, it is another way that many connected educators intentionally unplug.

Solitude   It may seem a bit ironic and counterintuitive to suggest that connected educators must intentionally plan for periods of solitude, yet we have actually found this to be the case for most successful people in general and connected educators specifically. Although they spend a huge percentage of their waking hours connected to other human beings, both face to face and through online interactions, connected educators also set aside time to spend alone with their thoughts. As is the case with both exercise and reading, time spent in solitude can look quite different depending on the individual person, the job they have, their family situations, and other variables. Some administrators and teachers we know close their classroom or office doors for a few minutes during the day to simply sit and think. Others start their day alone, engaging in quiet thought, prayer, or mentally walking through the day that awaits them. Still others end their day in much the same way, but in reflecting on the day that has passed, rather than plotting out the day that awaits. The fact remains that our professional lives tend to be somewhat hectic and filled with hundreds of interactions each day. We are faced with an endless number of decisions to make, meetings to attend, lessons to teach, trainings to plan, and online conversations in which to engage. The extent of this widespread connectivity makes it more important than ever to set time aside for being alone with our thoughts. Depending on our circumstances, these times of solitude may well be brief, yet they are critically important. Whether they carve out ten minutes of solitude to start their day, find several brief moments throughout the day to spend alone with their thoughts, or plan on extended periods of time alone to think, plan, and reflect, connected educators intentionally plan for time alone as another way to unplug.

▶ MULTITASK OR FOCUS?

Several years ago, it seemed as if the idea of *multitasking* was all the rage or, at a minimum, a necessary evil for anyone hoping to survive and accomplish everything that needed to be done in a given day, week, month, or school year. Originally, the term multitasking was used to refer to computers that could perform more than a single task simultaneously. Over time, the term became associated with human beings performing—or at least attempting to perform—more than one task at a time. Human multitasking is "the apparent performance by an individual of handling more than one task at the same time" (Human multitasking, 2014, para. 1). Although we still see many busy educators trying to save time by attempting to manage more than one task at the same time, we have rarely come across individuals who do so successfully as part of their routine work life. On the contrary, we have found that multitasking makes us less, rather than more, productive.

It is quite easy for busy educators to fall prey to the temptation of multitasking. In a typical school day, nary a minute passes when we are not faced with a number of items requiring our attention, whether we are classroom teachers, school administrators, counselors, or hold any other role within a school district. We have each attended many meetings in which those gathered were sitting with laptops open, attempting to focus on both what was being said at the meeting as well as something on their computer screen. Invariably, such people are not disinterested in the meeting nor are they disrespectful, disgruntled employees; instead, they tend to be extremely busy people hoping to accomplish two tasks at the same time. In our experiences, this is rarely an effective or efficient way to manage the tasks before us. Instead, we have found that connected educators focus on the task at hand rather than attempt to divide their attention among several tasks. Although it may prove efficient to do so at times for very brief tasks or for an extremely simple task requiring very little attention, we are almost never well served—nor, more importantly, are those we are serving—by trying to fully engage in two things at one time.

Studies have shown that multitasking simply does not work. One study showed that we experience a 40% drop in productivity when we multitask and that it actually takes us a longer amount of time to complete a single task (American Psychological Association, 2014). According to another study conducted by Stanford, people who are regularly faced with multiple streams of electronic information do not pay attention, control their memory, or switch from one job to another as well as those who prefer to complete one task at a time (Gorlick, 2009). Another study by Hamilton, Vohs, Sellier, and Meyvis (2011) found that different tasks called for different states of mind, called mindsets. In education, for example, dealing with a concerned parent on the phone requires a different mindset than reading an email from your principal. You do a better job, the researchers found, when you do as much as you can using one mindset before switching gears to another. The study measured the ability of workers to perform various mental exercises after spending time switching mindsets to complete different tasks. The effort of switching mindsets seemed to cause people mental exhaustion. People who did not have to switch mindsets often performed better on follow-up tests of mental ability. Connected educators are every bit as busy and are faced with as many tasks to accomplish as anyone in any other role. However, they know that they can accomplish more by focusing on the task at hand as opposed to attempting to accomplish two things—or more—at once. Whether they are focusing on a face-to-face conversation with a colleague, grading essays written by their students, or participating in a Twitter chat for an hour, they tend to focus on the single task at hand. They know that in the long run doing so actually saves them time and allows them to better attend to each task. Most important of all, perhaps, connected educators know that when they are connecting with another person in any format, whether in person or online, focusing 100% of their attention on the person or people with whom they are interacting is the right thing to do and models for others how they should behave.

▶ REFLECT, MONITOR, AND ADJUST

Connected educators are extremely busy human beings who are so passionate about their careers that they want to dedicate as much time as possible to learning more about how they can do a better job tomorrow than they did today. They willingly and eagerly take it upon themselves to make time outside the scope of their regular school day and role therein to work even more in the evenings, on weekends, and even on vacations to reach out to other educators in an effort to become better. They tend to possess an extraordinary amount of energy, enthusiasm, and passion and exude an aura of positivity in all that they do. However, like everyone else in the world, they are provided with only 24 hours in every day, seven days each week, 365 days each year. They know that there are limits to what they can manage in a given period of time. As a result, they intentionally and consciously choose to unplug as part of their daily and weekly routines.

Educators who spend a significant amount of time connecting with others beyond the walls of their own workplace realize that they are models for the colleagues and the students with whom they interact. They realize that part of digital citizenship is knowing not only when and how to connect, but also when and how to unplug. They realize that part of what they must model as connected educators is not spending too much time and energy being connected and that a key to success in any pursuit is balancing competing interests and demands upon our time. Successful educators who spend a great deal of time interacting with and

> **❝**Educators who spend a significant amount of time connecting with others beyond the walls of their own workplace realize that . . . part of digital citizenship is knowing not only when and how to connect, but also when and how to unplug.**❞**

learning with their members of their learning network make it a point to monitor their time spent in this manner to ensure that it is not encroaching on their social, emotional, or physical health or interfering with the relationships they have with their family, friends, or workplace colleagues. They set aside time to actually monitor how they spend their hours each week, reflecting on what they learned, what they accomplished, and also what was left unfinished. When they find that their lives are tilting out of balance in one direction, they take action to correct the imbalance. At times, connected educators know that this includes reaching the conclusion that to truly connect to the world around them requires intentionally *pulling the plug* on 24/7 connectivity. When you periodically unplug from technology, you are better able to effectively reconnect with yourself.

FOLLOW 5, FIND 5, TAKE 5

Follow 5: These five educators from our PLN stand as models in the areas we have written about in this chapter: never forgetting that ours is a hectic, stressful profession and that we must achieve balance and find time to unplug from our learning network. We have listed their names along with their Twitter "handles." We encourage you to follow these exemplary educators on Twitter and interact with them to enhance your life as a connected educator. Here are short insights from these experts in the field on the importance of unplugging and finding balance:

1. *Larry Ferlazzo (@Larryferlazzo)*. High school teacher, Sacramento, California. Larry is a prolific blogger, including Larry Ferlazzo's Websites of the Day at http://larryferlazzo.edublogs.org/; Classroom Q and A at http://blogs.edweek.org/teachers/classroom_qa_with_larry_ferlazzo/; Building Parent Engagement in School at http://engagingparentsinschool.edublogs.org/According to Ferlazzo,

Building a broad-based Personal Learning Network through social media is an extraordinarily effective way to hear about new resources, learn from so many other educators' successes and mistakes, and connect for "sister-class" projects all over the world. In addition, it can be an important avenue for developing educational policy issues and shining the light equally on those that promote justice and equity for our students and their families and those that do the opposite. That said, at the same time social media has a place in our lives, and must also be kept in its place. It is possible to have too much of a good thing if time and space is not also created for reflection and for real flesh-and-blood connection.

2. *Starr Sackstein (@MsSackstein)*. High school English teacher and author, Oceanside, New York. Starr also co-moderates #sunchat, #jerdchat, and #nyedchat. According to Sackstein,

Being a connected educator has changed my professional commitment to teaching, but it has also put a strain on my personal life at times. Finding balance between the two is essential or something will suffer. It's important to always put family first and make a concerted effort to shut the devices off at some point modeling for your kids that "face time" is really necessary for developing interpersonal skills. Be aware of the time you spend online and don't allow the virtual connections to become more real than the physical ones you've built your life around.

3. *Robert Schuetz (@Robert_Schuetz)*. Technology coordinator, Palatine, Illinois. Bob is a frequent participant in the following Twitter chats: #mnlead, #IAedchat, #iledchat, #edchat, #1to1techat, and #satchat. According to Schuetz,

Like many others, I have experienced a personal and professional rebirth as a result of connecting with other educators through a personal learning network (PLN). Connected educators frequently cite several key advantages of socially networked learning, including: personalization of learning, collaborative spirit, professional voice, global perspective, and most importantly, relationship building. However, like other activities that we find fulfilling and enjoyable, connecting with others digitally is best done in moderation. There are times when unplugging from our social networks is not only appropriate, but essential to our face-to-face relationships. Family dinners, walking our dogs with my wife, fishing, and exercising are examples of times when I go into "airplane mode." Unplugging gives us the opportunity to connect with our loved ones, reflect on our experiences, appreciate our natural surroundings, and listen attentively to messages from our souls. Striking a balance between connected and unconnected time is challenging, but the rewards can be substantial and everlasting.

4. *Dan Butler (@danpbutler)*. Principal, Epworth and Farley Elementary Schools, Iowa. According to Butler,

Becoming a connected educator has changed my professional career by allowing me to network with members of my Personal Learning Network (PLN) all across the globe 24 hours a day/7 days a week. I have gained access to incredible documents, instructional plans, and resources that I have applied to my school district, and have also shared items to assist others within my PLN. Twitter and other social media tools have created collaborative efforts with leaders in the field of education and allowed me to approach my daily work with a great deal of support.

Our work is too critical to take on alone, and I encourage all educators to become connected with social media tools. With so much accessibility, it is important to remember to unplug, in order to spend quality time with our families. The time that we get with our families can never be replaced.

5. *Jill Maraldo (@jmaraldo).* Associate Principal for Instruction; Buffalo Grove, Illinois. Jill moderates #iledchat Monday nights from 9:00–10:00 CST. According to Maraldo,

Being a connected educator has changed me as an administrator. It has guided my professional growth and learning, influenced my doctoral research, and expanded my professional learning network. When planning #iledchat, it was important for us to maintain a healthy work/life balance, so we selected a time "after the kids go to bed" to make it better for the moderator team. As a working mom, it is essential to model lifelong learning for our three kids, while still being able to be fully present for them when I am home. While using Twitter for professional learning has been and continues to be the best PD I participate in, it is just as important to maintain face-to-face relationships with both your family AND those educators around you. Time flies on Twitter, so make sure you set limits and "put the phone down" when your family and friends deserve your full attention, or you are doing both them and yourself a great disservice. Social media allows you to expand your horizons as an educator, but it's just as important to "act local" with those educators in your school/district, in order to bring back that new learning and effect change.

Find 5: We have found these five online resources to be particularly useful in reflecting on the importance of maintaining balance in our lives. These are links to resources that we have learned about via our own PLN and that we have used ourselves to improve some aspect of our personal or professional lives:

1. Why You Should Unplug by Katie Lepi at http://www.edudemic. com/why-you-should-unplug/.
2. The High Cost of Multi-Tasking (infographic) at http://www.inc. com/laura-montini/infographic/the-high-cost-of-multitasking. html
3. 12 Reasons to Stop Multitasking Now by Amanda MacMillan at http://www.health.com/health/gallery/0,,20707868,00.html
4. 8 Ways to Achieve Better Work–Life Balance by Jacquelyn Smith at http://www.forbes.com/sites/jacquelynsmith/2013/04/18/8-ways-to-achieve-better-work-life-balance/.
5. Unplugged, Reflected, and Recharged! by Drew Minnock at http://www.twoguysandsomeipads.com/2014/04/unplugged-reflected-and-recharged.html.

Take 5: We conclude each chapter by recommending five action steps you can take to get started or continue on your path as a connected educator. Here are five steps we suggest you take to ensure you maintain balance in your life by consciously scheduling time to unplug:

1. Build three five-minute slots into your "regular" work day during which to walk away from your desk or area where you spend most of your work day. Take a walk outside or around the hallways of your school simply as a way to move, stretch, and recharge.

2. Consider participating in the "National Day of Unplugging" which takes place for a 24-hour period starting on the first Friday in March each year. Find more information at http://nationaldayo funplugging.com/.

3. Set aside at least 15 minutes each day to read a book, newspaper, or magazine. Avoid the temptation of simply reading an article online or on your tablet. Balance the amount of text you read on a computer screen with traditional text.

4. Enroll in a class completely unrelated to anything you do at work. It need not be an ongoing class requiring a long-term commitment. Instead, take a one-night cooking class or pottery class. Try something you have never done before.

5. Set a goal for volunteering or engaging in a service project of some sort. If you are not already engaged in such work, start small and set a monthly goal of a few hours. Invite a colleague, friend, or family member to join you in this pursuit.

Connecting the Dots

Creativity is just connecting things.

Steve Jobs

The Partnership for 21st Century Skills (n.d.) created a framework for 21st-century learning in which the "4 Cs (Creativity, Communication, Collaboration and Critical Thinking," para. 3) are highlighted as student outcomes we must seek to elicit in order to prepare them properly for college and careers. Typically, when we think about the 4Cs of 21st-century learning, we do so with our students in mind, yet we believe that much like almost everything else in education, what is pertinent to and important for students is also pertinent to and important for educators. As 21st-century educators, we must focus on the 4 Cs in our own daily activities. We want our students attending our schools to be authentically and actively engaged in these college- and career-ready behaviors. For them to act in such ways, we need to model the way, learning from our own experiences, and passing this learning on to our students. We agree with Jobs that the first of these 4Cs, creativity, is all about connecting things. We would also suggest that the other three are all about connecting as well. When we *collaborate*, we are connecting with other people; when we *think critically*, we are connecting thoughts in our own minds to other thoughts and ideas we have or about which we are learning; when we *communicate*, we are clearly involved in connecting with people and ideas, sharing our own thoughts, reflecting on the thoughts of others, and making connections as a result of these exchanges.

In this book, we have described eight "Key Connectors," or intentional ways that highly connected educators act in order to grow and learn professionally so that they continue to serve their schools and their students in the best ways possible. It all starts with **connecting to a personal and professional learning network** as outlined in Chapter 1. No one can begin to incorporate any new ideas they learn into their professional practice until they first connect to other people who are resources for these ideas. Once they have begun **establishing their P²LN**, connected educators then realize they can learn beyond the walls of their own classrooms, schools, or districts and beyond the school-day hours, and **begin to learn what they want, when they want, and how they want**. When connecting through their P²LN, they focus on the three Cs so important in the lives of educators, consistently looking for new ways to **focus on communication, collaboration, and community**. Although connected educators take away many exciting new ideas to try in their own schools and classrooms, they tend to give more than they take and derive just as much joy and energy from the giving as they do from the taking. They not only possess the growth mindset of which Dweck (2006) wrote, by looking to take ideas from others that they think will help them grow, but also a **"giving mindset," knowing they will grow as much, if not more, by giving as they do by taking**. Connected educators are masterful at living in and making the most of the present while also keeping an eye out to the future. They connect what they did yesterday to what they are doing today—and what they think they may have to do tomorrow. Always looking forward in this way, **they strive to be tomorrow, today**. Connected educators we know who have truly benefitted from connecting, and benefitted others in return, always keep in mind that every successful connection begins with relationship-building. Even in the midst of daily new advances in technology which allow us to connect in ways that can be considered impersonal, **connected educators always focus on relationships, relationships, relationships**, regardless of the vehicle they are using to connect. **Connected educators model the way** for others, knowing that the way they behave will have an impact on whether those around them will also strive to become connected. Even if they are connected to thousands of other educators around the world, they do not lose sight of those immediately surrounding them in their home workplace and they make the time to support their co-workers by showing how getting connected can help them, making sure to do so in a non-threatening, patient, and servant-like manner. Finally, **connected educators know when to unplug** and make time to connect with themselves as well as their close family and friends in ways that require intentional unplugging for significant amounts of time. They are passionate about staying connected to their global P²LN and just as passionate about staying connected to the people, places, things, and ideas awaiting them in the immediate world right outside their doorstep. They know that like anything else in life, staying plugged in too much can be counterproductive to the ultimate goal of growing and learning.

We have noticed that connected educators who have discovered that connecting with others is both a productive and joyful way to enhance their professional lives find both the joy and the meaning in connecting. These educators come in all shapes and sizes, representing all races, nations, genders, languages, and any other demographic subgroup imaginable. Yet, they share an amazing amount of desires and behaviors in common. The key connectors described in this book are the ones that have stood out to us as most commonly held among our own P²LNs and the traits that we believe are most important for others entering the rewarding arena known as connected education.

▶ CONNECTING THE DOTS: PEOPLE FIRST

Although we concur with Steve Jobs's statement in the quote at the top of this chapter, suggesting that creativity is all about connecting "things," we suspect he would include "people" under the "things" umbrella, as we cannot truly be creative in isolation. To create, we must connect with others. Creativity is sparked by connecting with other people. Oftentimes, connecting with one person leads to connecting to others, and before too long, this process compounds exponentially and quickly we become connected to an entire network of other people, each of whom is then connected to each other, in some degree. A seemingly haphazard collection of individuals in fact shares a larger bond in common.

When we were young, most of us played a game called "Connect the Dots," where you drew lines from one dot to another to another until you had created a "whole," a picture of something recognizable, from a series of scattered, seemingly random, dots on a page. In the previous eight chapters of this book, we highlighted educators from our P²LN as ones to follow in the "Follow 5" feature. After initially reaching out to them to gain their insights into specific aspects of connected education, we decided to go back and ask each of them: *Who connected you? If you had to list only one person, who was the person most responsible for getting you started on the oath to connectivity?* We started by asking the question of ourselves. Todd said it was most likely Jeff, during a time they were collaborating on another project. Jimmy said it was Jim Wichman. For Jeff, the person who encouraged (even badgered!) him to connect was Nancy Blair. To be completely honest, each of us had to be convinced that taking this next step in our educational journey would be worthwhile. We were all extremely busy already and were dubious that the extra time and effort we would be putting into this venture would be worth it in terms of any tangible benefits. Several years later, we are convinced that it completely changed and re-energized us as educators and as human beings, helping us to learn more than we ever could have done had we not taken this leap of faith.

We were curious to find out who connected our learning network colleagues we have highlighted throughout this book. Most of these connected educators have been connected for many years and together they have hundreds of thousands of educators around the globe who follow them on Twitter as a way to learn from and interact with them. They have been so successful for so long as connected educators, we wondered if they would even recall how they first got started. To our mild surprise, each of the 50 immediately replied, typically with an anecdote about where and when this nudge to get connected occurred, as well as by whom. We share the following list with you to show that each of these well-established educators started at ground zero. If you are reading this book as an educator who is just now pursuing an interest in this area, know that we have all been at that point and we are all thrilled we stuck with, it is due to the learning we have acquired, the relationships we have established, and the experiences we have shared. Every educator on this list below fervently agrees that getting connected has enhanced their lives and careers and they are extremely grateful to the person listed beside their name, who originally encouraged them to connect:

Jenna Shaw

Todd Neselony

Joe Sanfelippo

Cristina Zimmerman

Bill Ferriter

Joe Mazza

Tom Murray

Maria Galanis

Daisy Dyer Duerr

Lauren Taylor

Curt Rees

Tom Whitford

Arin Kress

Chris Kesler

Pernille Ripp

Paul Solarz

Erin Klein

Garnet Hillman

Marcie Faust

Nancy Blair

Dominique Dynes

Maggie Bolado

Dave Burgess

Matt Townsley

George Couros

Tara Copeman

John Wink

Dennis Schug

Rick Wormeli

Jennie Magiera

Joe Clark

John Carver

Salome Thomas-El

Amber Teamann

Brad Currie

Jill Maraldo

Robert Schuetz

Starr Sackstein

Larry Ferlazzo

Dan Butler

Shelly Blake-Pollack

Troy Mooncy

Todd Whitaker

Kara Jacobs

Dean Shareski

Eric Sheninger

Rich Kiker

Jeff Zoul

Eric Sheninger

Starr Sackstein

John Pederson

George Couros

Erin Klein

Todd Nesloney

Edna Sackson

Caz Badynee

Tony Vincent

Joy Kirr

Alan November

Bill Ferriter

Wendy Gorton

Asael Ruvalcaba

Dan McDowell

Russ Goerend

Alec Couros

Ewan McIntosh

Bill Ferriter

Jennifer Hogan

Brenda Dyck

Chad Kafka

Todd Whitaker

Tom Whitby

Brad Currie

George Couros

Eric Sheninger

Will Richardson

Tom Whitby

Joey Goodman

John Norton

Jimmy Casas

We suspect that many, if not all, of our P²LN colleagues listed above had no real idea what they were getting into when they first dipped their toes into the realm of connected education. Like you, perhaps, they may have been hesitant, even resistant, to get started. They likely had a multitude of excuses as to why they could not or should not devote the time to this new venture. They may have even scoffed at the idea at some point in their professional lives. Regardless of their initial attitudes, however, each of these educators is now passionately committed to continuing to seek new ways to connect with educators around the world as a way to improve their own professional lives as well as the lives of the educators with whom they are connected and the students they serve. Wherever you are currently on your journey to connectivity as an educator, we encourage you to take the next step; it is a giant step forward in your professional life.

▶ CONNECTING THE DOTS: IDEAS NEXT

Getting connected to other educators around the world is actually quite fun once you learn how to go about creating a learning network and begin interacting with members of your network. However, if it were only about meeting new colleagues and having fun, we doubt that anyone would continue along this path for long. What keeps connected educators energized about their learning network is not only the people with whom they connect, but also the ideas they get connected to, ideas that help them get better at what they do so that their students will have, as our P²LN member says, "a better tomorrow than they had today" (T. Murray, personal communication, July 14, 2014).

With knowledge so readily accessible in today's technological society, it is no longer the case that any one person has (or needs) the answers to all of life's questions or that any single individual is the smartest person in the room. Instead, we have reached a point whereby the smartest person in the room is not a person at all, but the room itself, meaning the collective wisdom of all who are gathered together, whether face to face in an actual room or connected together in a virtual room of some sort. The ideas we can brainstorm together are larger in number and higher in quality than the ideas we can generate alone. To gain access to the best ideas in education today—and to share your own voice, offering ideas that you have seen work—you must be connected beyond your immediate network of colleagues. We will not be able to do all that we can for the students we ultimately serve if we are not willing to look outside, as well as within, our own organizations.

Wiseman and McKeown (2010) argued for shifting away from being a *genius* (trying to be the smartest person in the room) to instead becoming a *genius maker* (using their intelligence to access and multiply the genius of others). Connected educators are poised to make just such a shift in the field of education, accessing the genius of learning network members and, in turn, empowering them to become even more impactful. Instead of trying to walk into a room (actual or virtual) and show how smart they are, connected educators—like Wiseman's multipliers—know that such an approach only serves to lower the shared IQ in the room, causing ideas to die and energy to sap. As a result, they apply their own intelligence in a different way, a way that amplifies the intelligence and capability of everyone around them while at the same time letting those around them learn from them and notice the effect they, too, are having on the room. According to Wiseman and McKeown (2010), when they were around multipliers,

> People got smarter and better in their presence. Ideas grew; challenges were surmounted; hard problems solved. When these leaders walked into a room, light bulbs started going off over people's heads. Ideas flew so fast that you had to replay the meeting in slow motion just to see what was going on. Meetings with them were mash-up sessions. These leaders seemed to make everyone around them better and more capable. These leaders weren't just intelligent themselves—they were intelligence Multipliers.
>
> (p. 5)

Connected educators are education's version of intelligence multipliers—with the caveat that in any given situation the connected educator acting as the primary multiplier can change; every active member of a P²LN is an intelligence multiplier, sharing their own wisdom, stealing the wisdom of others, building their own capacity, growing the capacity of others, multiplying *each other's* intelligence. The network member who shares an idea that works during one Twitter chat, for example, and sparks several other ideas in return, may be the same network member at an Edcamp that weekend who is inspired and gains wisdom from listening to another network member share a different idea which is totally new to him or her at that point in time. Connected educators understand—like Wiseman's multipliers understand—that how much you know is not what matters if you are trying to learn, grow, and be the best you can be. What matters is how much access you have to what other people know and how you can use that knowledge to create new ideas which help you in your own setting. Connected educators are constantly seeking to find new ideas as well as share their own ideas, connecting what they already know with something they recently learned and at the same time, connecting their learning network members with ideas they think will help them in their own quest.

▶ CONNECTING THE DOTS: ENDING WHERE WE STARTED

We hope that many people reading this book already consider themselves to be connected educators; for them, we hope that the ideas we have discussed in this book have validated their own thoughts and behaviors and have sparked at least a few additional ideas about the importance of remaining connected. We also hope that many readers are educators who currently are not connected or are only just beginning on their journey to connectivity. To you, we encourage you to press on in your journey, knowing that if you stay the course, you will find it a course well worth pursuing. We also ask you to connect with us, following us via Twitter, emailing us, or calling us whenever you have an idea to share or a question to ask. As educators who have benefitted immensely from the collective wisdom of our own learning networks, nothing brings us more joy than returning the favor whenever we are able.

At the outset of this book, we stated that serving as a connected educator is more of a mindset than a skill set. It is not so much about what you know and are able to do as it is about who you are and how you behave, including living out the eight key connectors emphasized in this book as characteristics of connected educators. Our abbreviated definition of connected educators as *ones who are actively and constantly seeking new opportunities and resources to grow as professionals* says it all: they do not have all the answers, nor will they ever be as good as they want to be, but they will leave no stone uncovered in an effort to serve students better tomorrow than they did today. In addition to beginning this book by writing about what a connected educator is, we also stated that it is important to start with asking why it matters. As we stated in the preface, the "why?" varies only slightly among all connected educators with whom we have worked and boils down to a relentless desire to find out how they can be better at what they do in order to better serve their students.

The average day in the life of every educator in the world is one that, from start to finish, is filled with a literal flurry of activities, duties, responsibilities, decisions, problems, conflicts, events, meetings, phone calls, and emails, to name but a few of the many things that consume our ever-so-precious allotment of time. Everywhere we go, educators joke about not even having time to use the restroom or eat lunch, and often times, the joke is more of a reality than it is a joke. As ridiculously busy educators ourselves, we know just how busy you are and we would be lying if we said that becoming a connected educator will require no additional time from your already depleted store. It will require time. It will also require patience to see the results. But if you stay the course, we promise that eventually you will begin to understand that by connecting the dots, you will begin to transform these individual pockets of excellence into a network of excellence.

If you began upon this journey years ago, congratulations on leading the way. If you have yet to start the journey, it is not too late. In fact, starting today would be an ideal time to start. Do not wait until tomorrow. Start small, perhaps by setting aside 20–30 minutes, four or five times a week, to connect with like-minded educators. Some days, you will find yourself on a roll of extremely worthwhile interactions and find that your 20 minutes turned into an hour or more of time invested in connecting. On other occasions, you may find that all you can do is tweet out a quick quote that you like or a single photo of something that happened in your classroom. Start small. Stay the course. Share your story. Reap the benefits that are sure to come your way as a result. Your professional and personal life will be enriched by doing so. Each morning, Jeff sends out a short tweet exhorting those in his learning network to "Work Hard . . . Have Fun . . . Be Nice . . . Today!" When you are surrounded by an active P²LN, you will find yourself surrounded and supported by a host of people who work hard, who have fun, and who are nice . . . each and every day! Their hard work, fun-loving attitudes, and kind natures will help to make your bad days less bad and your good days even better. You, in turn, will do the same for them. And, together, we will all become smarter and better at what we do because two heads tend to be better than one, three is better still, and so it goes. To paraphrase the words of a quote typically attributed to Woodrow Wilson, we must use not only all the brains we have, but also all the brains we can borrow. Our work is too important to not use all the brainpower available to us. By entering into the world of connected education, we can contribute our own brainpower to the world while learning from the best and the brightest currently serving in the noblest profession of all: the education of our youth.

References

#hashtags.org (2014). Organizing the world's hashtags. Retrieved from https://www.hashtags.org/ (accessed 17 July 2014).

American Psychological Association (2014). *Multitasking: Switching Costs.* Washington, DC: Author. Retrieved from http://www.apa.org/research/action/multitask.aspx (accessed 17 October 2014).

Barth. R. S. (2006). Improving relationships within the schoolhouse. *Educational Leadership, 63*(6), 8–13. Retrieved from http://www.ascd.org/publications/educational-leadership/mar06/vol63/num06/Improving-Relationships-Within-the-Schoolhouse.aspx (accessed 17 October 2014).

Bryk, A. S., & Schneider, B. (2002). *Trust in Schools: A Core Resource for Improvement.* New York, NY: Sage Foundation.

Bulka, M. (2013). A student's perspective. [Blog post.] Retrieved from http://leydenlearn365.blogspot.com/2014/02/leydenpride-student-perspective.html (accessed 17 October 2014).

Burgess, D. (2012). *Teach Like a Pirate.* San Diego, CA: Dave Burgess Consulting.

Casas, Jimmy (2013, November 17). Passion . . . purpose . . . pride. [Blog post.] Retrieved from http://jimmycasas.blogspot.com/2013_11_01_archive.html (accessed 17 October 2014).

Clarke, J. H. (2003). Changing systems to personalized learning: Personalized learning. Providence, RI: The Education Alliance at Brown University. Retrieved from http://www.brown.edu (accessed 17 October 2014).

Cocotas, A. (2013, May 20). 88% of U.S. consumers use mobile as second screen while watching TV. *Business Insider.* Retrieved from http://www.businessinsider.com/a-majority-uses-mobile-as-second-screen-2013–5 (accessed 17 October 2014).

Cornelius-White, J. (2007). Learner-centered teacher–student relationships are effective: A meta-analysis. *Review of Educational Research, 77*(1), 113–143. doi:10.3102/003465430298563.

Currie, B. (2014, May 25). Take action. [Blog post.] Retrieved from http://www.bradcurrie.net/blog/taking-action (accessed 17 October 2014).

Dachis, A. (2012, January 24). Which blogging platform should I use? [Blog post.] Retrieved from http://lifehacker.com/5878847/which-blogging-platform-should-i-use (accessed 17 October 2014).

Dweck, C. (2006). *Mindset: The New Psychology of Success.* New York, NY: Random House.

Edcamp (2014). Complete edcamp calendar. Retrieved from http://edcamp.wikispaces.com?Complete+edcamp+calendar (accessed 17 October 2014).

Edcamp Foundation (n.d.). How to edcamp. Retrieved from http://edcamp.org/how-to-edcamp/ (accessed 17 October 2014).

Edcamp Foundation (2012). Why edcamp? Retrieved from http://edcamp.org/wp-content/uploads/2012/07/Edcamp_Whitepaper_Executive_Summary.pdf (accessed 17 October 2014).

Educational Technology and Mobile Learning (2013). A simple guide on the use of hashtag for teachers. Retrieved from http://www.educatorstechnology.com/2013/05/a-simple-guide-on-use-of-hashtag-for.html (accessed 17 October 2014).

EduTechers Change the World (2012). Change the world campaign—2012. [Blog post.] Retrieved from https://www.youtube.com/watch?v=3yh5gVCx0LA (accessed 17 October 2014).

Enquist, S. (2013). 33% rule. [Video file.] Retrieved from https://www.youtube.com/watch?v=SXQ2MdlwHrI (accessed 17 October 2014).

Fitzgerald, B. (2012, July 10). Social media is causing anxiety, study finds. *Huffington Post.* Retrieved from http://www.huffingtonpost.com/2012/07/10/social-media-anxiety_n_1662224.html (accessed 17 October 2014).

Freedman, G. (2009, July 13). *From an Education Pipeline to Cycles of Learning: Is the Tipping Point for Education in Sight?* Washington, DC: Blackboard Institute. Retrieved from http://www.blackboardinstitute.com/pdf/Tipping_Point_WhitePaper.pdf (accessed 17 October 2014).

Fullan, M. (2001). *Leading in a Culture of Change.* San Francisco, CA: Jossey-Bass. Retrieved from http://www.files.eric.ed.gov/fulltext/ED467449.pdf (accessed 17 October 2014).

Fullan, M. (2014). *The Principal.* San Francisco: CA: Jossey-Bass.

Gardner, H. (2010, July 14). Personalize and deliver. [Blog post.] Retrieved from http://gettingsmart.com/2010/07/personalize-learning-to-broaden-equity-and-knowledge/ (accessed 17 October 2014).

Goleman, D., Boyatzis, R., & McKee, A. (2002). *Primal Leadership: Realizing the Power of Emotional Intelligence* (1st edn.). Boston, MA: Harvard Business Press.

Gorlick, A. (2009). Media multitaskers pay mental price, Stanford study shows. *Stanford News.* Retrieved from http://news.stanford.edu/news/2009/august24/multitask-research-study-082409.html (accessed 17 October 2014).

Grant, A. (2014, March 17). How to succeed professionally by help-ing others. *The Atlantic.* Retrieved from http://www.theatlantic. com/health/archive/2014/03/how-to-succeed-professionally-by-helping-others/284429/ (accessed 17 October 2014).

Grant, A.M. (2013). *Give and Take: A Revolutionary Approach to Suc-cess.* New York, NY: Viking Adult.

Graziano, C. (2005, February 9). Public education faces a crisis in teacher retention. Retrieved from http://www.edutopia.org/new-teacher-burnout-retention (accessed 17 October 2014).

Hamilton, R., Vohs, K.D., Sellier, A.L., & Meyvis, T. (2011). Being of two minds: Switching mindsets impairs subsequent functioning of mind. *Organizational Behavior and Human Decision Processes, 115*, 13–24. doi:10.1016/j.obhdp.2010.11.005.

Hersey, P., & Blanchard, K. (1985). *The Situational Leader.* New York, NY: Warner Books.

Hersey, P., Blanchard, K.H., & Johnson, D.E. (2007). *Management of Organizational Behavior: Leading Human Resources* (9th edn.). Up-per Saddle River, NJ: Prentice Hall.

"Human multitasking" (2014). Wikipedia, the free encyclopedia. [On-line.] Retrieved from http://en.wikipedia.org/wiki/Human_multi tasking (accessed 17 October 2014).

Kouzes, J.M., & Posner, B.Z. (2003a). *Encouraging the Heart: A Lead-er's Guide to Rewarding and Recognizing Others.* San Francisco, CA: Jossey-Bass.

Kouzes, J.M., & Posner, B.Z. (2003b). *The Leadership Challenge* (3rd edn.). San Francisco, CA: Jossey-Bass.

Lewin, R., & Regine, B. (2000). *The Soul at Work: Embracing Complex-ity Science for Business Success.* New York, NY: Simon & Schuster.

Markey, J. (2012). Where is your school's online conversation? [Blog post.] Retrieved from http://jmarkeyap.blogspot.com/2012/11/ where-is-your-schools-online.html?view=sidebar (accessed 17 Oc-tober 2014).

Marzano, R.J., Waters, T., & McNulty, B.A. (2005). *School Leadership That Works: From Research to Results.* Alexandria, VA: Association for Supervision and Curriculum Development.

Mazza, J. (2014, April 22). *T.H.E.* journal's innovator of the month with executive editor Chris Piehler and J. [Blog post.] Retrieved from http://www.blogtalkradio.com/edutalk/2014/04/22/the-journals-innovator-of-the-month-with-executive-editor-chris-piehler-and-j (accessed 17 October 2014).

McLeod, S. (2011, January 28). Some big questions for educators (and parents and policymakers). [Blog post.] Retrieved from http://dan gerouslyirrelevant.org/2011/01 (accessed 17 October 2014).

Murray, T. (2013, March 13). The power of Twitter chats. [Blog post.] Retrieved from https://www.youtube.com/watch?feature=player_embedded&v=brI8sHmg89w (accessed 17 October 2014).

National Sleep Foundation (2011, March 7). Annual sleep in America poll exploring connections with communications technology use and sleep. Washington, DC: Author. Retrieved from http://sleep foundation.org/media-center/press-release/annual-sleep-america-poll-exploring-connections-communications-technology-use-(accessed 17 October 2014).

November Learning (n.d.). Popular education hashtags on Twitter. Retrieved from https://docs.google.com/a/dps109.org/document/d/1Rzv0_q0jPsa5LIzgQ7OQBQ8DNyEEzbZWF3MvHP7yahI/edit?pli=1 (accessed 17 October 2014).

Office of Career, Technical, and Adult Education (2013). Celebrating connected educator month 2013. Washington, DC: U.S. Department of Education. Retrieved from http://www.ed.gov/edblogs/ovae/2013/10/23/celebrating-connected-educator-month-2013/ (accessed 17 October 2014).

Partnership for 21st Century Skills (n.d.). *Framework for 21st century learning.* Washington, DC: Author. Retrieved from http://www.p21. org/about-us/p21-framework (accessed 17 October 2014).

Perez, S. (2013, January 7). Nielsen: TV still king in media consumption; only 16 percent of TV homes have tablets. *Tech Crunch Daily.* Retrieved from http://techcrunch.com/2013/01/07/nielsen-tv-still-king-in-media-consumption-only-16-percent-of-tv-homes-have-tablets/ (accessed 17 October 2014).

Richtel, M. (2010, June 7). Attached to technology and paying a price. *New York Times.* Retrieved from http://www.nytimes.com/2010/06/07/technology/07brain.html?pagewanted=all&_r=0 (accessed 17 October 2014).

Roberts, J. A., & Pirog, S. F., III (2012). Preliminary investigation of materialism and impulsiveness as predictors of technological addictions among young adults. *Journal of Behavioral Addictions,* 2(1), 56–62. doi:10.1556/JBA.1.2012.011.

Schneiderman, M. (2010, June 27). Personalized learning central to whole child approach. [Guest blog by Judy Seltz.] Retrieved from http://www.siia.net/blog/index.php/2010/06/personalized-learning-central-to-whole-child-approach/ (accessed 17 October 2014).

Sebring, P., & Bryk, A. (2000). Principal leadership and the bottom line in Chicago. *Phi Delta Kappan, 81*(5). Retrieved from https://ccsr.uchicago.edu/sites/default/files/publications/SchoolLeadershipAndTheBottomLine.pdf (accessed 17 October 2014).

Silva, G. (2013, September 25). Student hacking suspends LAUSD iPad program. Retrieved from http://www.myfoxla.com/story/23527759/student-hacking-suspends-lausd-ipad-program (accessed 17 October 2014).

Simple K12. (n.d.). The complete guide: How to start & run your very own EdCamp. Retrieved from http://webcache.googleusercontent.com/search?q=cache:-NMhQlc5dxYJ:edcamp.wikispaces.com/file/view/HowToEdCamp.pdf+&cd=1&hl=en&ct=clnk&gl=us (accessed 17 October 2014).

Sinek, S. (2011). *Start With Why: How Great Leaders Inspire Everyone to Take Action.* New York, NY: Penguin Books.

Sinek, S. (2013, September 29). Start with why. [Web log comment.] Retrieved from https://www.youtube.com/watch?v=sioZd3AxmnE (accessed 17 October 2014).

Smith, A. (2012). The best (and worst) of mobile connectivity. Washington, DC: Pew Research Center. Retrieved from http://www.pewinternet.org/2012/11/30/the-best-and-worst-of-mobile-connectivity/ (accessed 17 October 2014).

Swanson, K. (2013, April 23). Why edcamp? Retrieved from http://www.edutopia.org/blog/why-edcamp-kristen-swanson (accessed 17 October 2014).

TED.com. (n.d.). Ideas worth spreading. Retrieved from http://www.ted.com/ (accessed 17 October 2014).

The Weekly Twitter Chat Times (n.d.). The weekly Twitter chat schedule. Retrieved from https://docs.google.com/a/dps109.org/spreadsheet/ccc?key=0AiftIdjCeWSXdDRLRzNsVktUUGJpRWJhdUlWLS1Genc#gid=0 (accessed 17 October 2014).

Tschannen-Moran, M., & Hoy, W.K. (1998). Trust in schools: A conceptual and empirical analysis. *Journal of Educational Administration, 36,* 334–352. doi:10.1108/09578239810211518.

"Using hashtags on Twitter" (2014). Retrieved from https://support.twitter.com/articles/49309-using-hashtags-on-twitter# (accessed 17 October 2014).

Whitaker, T. (2002). *What Great Principals Do Differently.* New York, NY: Routledge.

Whitaker, T. (2004). *What Great Teachers Do Differently.* New York, NY: Routledge.

Whitaker, T., & Zoul, J. (2008). *4 CORE Factors for School Success.* New York, NY: Routledge.

Wiseman, L., & McKeown, G. (2010). *Multipliers: How the Best Leaders Make Everyone Smarter.* New York, NY: Harper Business.

World Wide Web Foundation (2014). History of the web. Retrieved from http://webfoundation.org/about/vision/history-of-the-web/ (accessed 17 October 2014).